KV-191-275

What to avoid.. 67

Does diet have much effect on this condition?.. 72

Other treatment options............................... 74

Summary 75

Hemochromatosis Diet 77

What You Need to Know About Diet & Nutrition in
Hemochromatosis 78

Important Considerations to Keep in Mind for a
Hemochromatosis Diet 80

The Most Important Foods To Avoid When You
Have Hemochromatosis................................. 81

Iron-Rich Foods to Limit in Hemochromatosis... 83

Iron-Fortified Foods and the Dangers for Hemochromatosis Patients.............................. 87

Non-Iron Nutrients That Impact Iron Overload in Hemochromatosis 90

Top Iron Enhancers: Foods that Make Iron Overload Worse in Hemochromatosis 92

Top Iron Blockers: Foods that Limit Iron Absorption in Hemochromatosis 93

A Diet Helpful for Hemochromatosis 94

Healthy And Easy Home-made Recipes............ 97

Invigorating Lemon Iced Tea Recipe 97

Hot Toddy Tea Recipe................................. 100

Acai Juice Recipe 102

Contents

Hemochromatosis 18

Symptoms 19

When to see a doctor 21

Causes 22

How hemochromatosis affects your organs 24

Hereditary hemochromatosis isn't the only type of

hemochromatosis. Other types include: 26

Risk factors 28

Complications 29

Diagnosis 31

Additional testing 34

Treatment 37

Lifestyle and home remedies 41

Preparing for your appointment 42

What you can do 43

Questions to ask your doctor 45

What to expect from your doctor 46

There are two types of this condition -- primary and secondary... 49

Symptoms.. 50

Diagnosis 53

Treatment.. 56

Hemochromatosis diet.................................. 58

Dietary factors.. 60

What to eat.. 62

Classic Falafels: The Vegan, Fried Fritters ... 103

Traditional Dolma Recipe 109

Piping Hot Turkish Tea Recipe 116

Delicious Homemade Matcha Green Tea Frappuccino 119

Middle Eastern Pita Bread Recipe 122

How To Make Sour Milk 125

Hong Kong Milk Tea 127

How To Make Golden Syrup At Home 129

How To Make Poppy Seed Tea 132

How to Make Clove Oil: Easy Steps 135

How to Make Ayahuasca Tea At Home 137

Okra Water Recipe 140

How to Make Orange Lemonade With Mint &
Ginger 143

Mixed Berry Salad Recipe 145

Roasted Breadfruit Recipe 146

How To Cook Shirataki Noodles 149

The Best Coconut Flour Recipe 151

Stuffed Summer Squash............................ 154

Fried Potatoes & Ramps Recipe 158

French Onion Soup 160

A Simple Glazed Carrot Recipe.................. 164

Oatmeal Deluxe....................................... 166

Spinach, Egg, and Quinoa Breakfast.......... 168

Sweet Potato Hash 170

Banana Bread Muffins 172

Hit The Spot Hot Chocolate 174

Toasted Almond Smoothie......................... 176

Spelt Pancakes 177

Healthiest Pancakes Ever 179

Homemade Greek Yogurt 181

Homestyle Turkey Sausage 184

Peanut Butter Banana Protein Shake 186

Clean French Toast................................... 188

Breakfast Bars... 190

Fiesta Scrambled Eggs 193

Slow Cooker Apple and Cinnamon Steel Cut Oats
.... 195

Homemade Muesli 197

Indian Beef with Spaghetti Squash............. 199

Italian Sausage Stuffed Portobello Mushrooms
.... 202

Curried Chicken Salad 205

Turkey Chili.. 208

Dynomite Sloppy Joes............................... 211

Steak and Pepper Crunch Salad 213

Coconut Chicken Tenders........................... 215

Baked Whitefish 217

Melt in Your Mouth Chicken....................... 218

Turkey Meatball Cauliflower....................... 220

Broiled Mexican Salmon 223

Pan Baked Salmon.................................... 225

Spicy Honey Chicken Thighs...................... 229

Lemon Garlic Cod 231

Zesty Lemon Chicken............................... 233

Tuscan Meatballs.................................... 236

Italian Fried Chicken Bites 239

Easy Crockpot Chicken 241

Easy Lemon Chicken 242

Asian Stir Fry 245

Rosemary Garlic Chicken........................... 247

Best Ever Burgers.................................... 249

Roasted Eggplant and Asparagus............... 251

Spinach and Feta Turkey Burgers............... 253

Beef with Veggies..................................... 255

Sheet Pan Italian Chicken Dinner 257

Hearty Italian Beef and Vegetable Soup 259

Quick and Easy Italian Meatballs................ 263

Hearty Italian Beef and Vegetable Soup 267

Easy Beef Lasagna.................................... 271

Crawfish Étouffée 277

Pressure Cooker Moroccan Chicken............ 280

Sheet Pan English Breakfast Recipe............ 286

Sheet Pan Fish and Chips Recipe 293

Chicken Mulligatawny Soup 299

Náutica Tropical Smoothie Recipe 304

Black Bean And Mango Salsa..................... 305

Hearty Burrito Bowls 311

Baked Shrimp Salmon 316

Spring Detox Cauliflower Salad 319

Detox Chicken Soup................................. 322

Philly Cheese Steak Stuffed Bell Peppers 325

Garlic Parmesan Baked Carrot Fries............ 328

Spice-Roasted Salmon With Roasted Cauliflower

.... 331

Greek Salad Wraps 334

Slim AM Jello Pops................................... 336

Watermelon Pizza 338

Poached Egg On Avocado Toast 340

Spring Salad with Slim AM dressing............ 342

Roasted Red Pepper Mozzarella And Basil Stuffed Chicken 345

Veggie And Hummus Sandwich.................. 348

Salmon Salad-Stuffed Avocado 349

Pizza Omelette 351

Brick-Oven Pizza (Brooklyn Style).............. 353

Turkey Bolognese Sauce 358

Grilled Tuna Teriyaki................................ 360

Elegant Pork Loin Roast 362

Szechwan Shrimp 366

Ginger Glazed Mahi Mahi.......................... 369

Chicken with Garlic, Basil, and Parsley........ 371

Chinese Pork Chops 374

Honey-Dijon Chicken With A Kick 376

Portobello Mushroom Caps and Veggies 378

Grilled Pork Tenderloin 380

Spicy Basil Chicken 382

Homemade Black Bean Veggie Burgers 384

Hawaiian Chicken Kabobs 387

Mustard Crusted Tilapia 390

Pesto Pasta 392

California Melt 394

Fluffy French Toast 396

Amazing Pork Tenderloin in the Slow Cooker

.... 398

Black Beans and Rice 400

Fish in Foil 402

Blackened Chicken 404

Pesto Pasta with Chicken 407

Easy Baked Tilapia 409

Baked Honey Mustard Chicken 411

RamJam Chicken 414

Ginger Veggie Stir-Fry 417

Apple Cinnamon Oatmeal 420

Red Lentil Curry 421

Turkey Veggie Meatloaf Cups 424

Lemon Garlic Tilapia 427

Chicken Kabobs 429

Spicy Chicken Breasts 434

Spaghetti Squash I 436

Easy Slow Cooker Meatballs 439

Ginger Glazed Mahi Mahi.......................... 441

Garlic Shrimp Linguine 444

Utokia's Ginger Shrimp and Broccoli with Garlic

.... 447

Mediterranean Chicken 450

Slow Cooker Cilantro Lime Chicken 453

Easy Cola Chicken 455

Porridge... 457

Jamaican Jerk Chicken 458

Chicken in a Pot 462

Leftover Chicken Croquettes...................... 465

Steelhead Trout Bake with Dijon Mustard ... 467

Braised Balsamic Chicken 469

Chicken Satay 471

Maple-Garlic Marinated Pork Tenderloin...... 473

Fiery Fish Tacos with Crunchy Corn Salsa ... 476

Grilled Asian Ginger Pork Chops................. 479

Easy Garlic and Rosemary Chicken............. 481

Slow Cooker Chicken Cacciatore 483

Pineapple Chicken Tenders........................ 484

Pineapple Pork Chops 487

Eggless Pasta... 489

Broccoli Beef I.. 492

Cod with Italian Crumb Topping 494

Chickpea Curry 496

Fast and Friendly Meatballs 499

Quick Black Beans and Rice 501

Slow Cooker Chicken Marrakesh 504

Spicy Tuna Sushi Roll 506

Bengali Chicken Curry with Potatoes 510

Baked Halibut Steaks 513

Fra Diavolo Sauce With Pasta 516

Hemochromatosis

Hereditary hemochromatosis (he-moe-kroe-muh-TOE-sis) causes your body to absorb too much iron from the food you eat. Excess iron is stored in your organs, especially your liver, heart and pancreas. Too much iron can lead to life-threatening conditions, such as liver disease, heart problems and diabetes.

The genes that cause hemochromatosis are inherited, but only a minority of people who have the genes ever develop serious problems. Signs and symptoms of hereditary hemochromatosis usually appear in midlife.

Treatment includes regularly removing blood from your body. Because much of the body's iron is contained in red blood cells, this treatment lowers iron levels.

Symptoms

Some people with hereditary hemochromatosis never have symptoms. Early signs and symptoms often overlap with those of other common conditions.

Signs and symptoms may include:

Joint pain

Abdominal pain

Fatigue

Weakness

Diabetes

Loss of sex drive

Impotence

Heart failure

Liver failure

Bronze or gray skin color

Memory fog

When signs and symptoms typically appear

Hereditary hemochromatosis is present at birth. But most people don't experience signs and symptoms until later in life — usually after the age of 40 in men and after age 60 in women. Women are more likely to develop symptoms after menopause, when they no longer lose iron with menstruation and pregnancy.

When to see a doctor

See your doctor if you experience any of the signs and symptoms of hereditary hemochromatosis. If you have an immediate family member who has hemochromatosis, ask your doctor about genetic tests that can determine if you have inherited the gene that increases your risk of hemochromatosis.

Causes

Hereditary hemochromatosis is caused by a mutation in a gene that controls the amount of iron your body absorbs from the food you eat. These mutations are passed from parents to children. This type of hemochromatosis is by far the most common type.

Gene mutations that cause hemochromatosis

A gene called HFE is most often the cause of hereditary hemochromatosis. You inherit one HFE gene from each of your parents. The HFE gene has two common mutations, C282Y and H63D. Genetic testing can reveal whether you have these mutations in your HFE gene.

If you inherit 2 abnormal genes, you may develop hemochromatosis. You can also pass the mutation on to your children. But not everyone who inherits two genes develops problems linked to the iron overload of hemochromatosis.

If you inherit 1 abnormal gene, you're unlikely to develop hemochromatosis. However, you are considered a gene mutation carrier and can pass the mutation on to your children. But your children wouldn't develop the disease unless they also inherited another abnormal gene from the other parent.

How hemochromatosis affects your organs

Iron plays an essential role in several body functions, including helping in the formation of blood. But too much iron is toxic.

A hormone called hepcidin, secreted by the liver, normally controls how iron is used and absorbed in the body, as well as how excess iron is stored in various organs. In hemochromatosis, the normal role of hepcidin is disrupted, causing your body to absorb more iron than it needs.

This excess iron is stored in major organs, especially your liver. Over a period of years, the stored iron can cause severe damage that may lead to organ failure and chronic diseases, such as cirrhosis, diabetes and heart failure. Though many people have faulty genes that cause hemochromatosis, not everyone develops iron overload to a degree that causes tissue and organ damage.

Hereditary hemochromatosis isn't the only type of hemochromatosis. Other types include:

Juvenile hemochromatosis. This causes the same problems in young people that hereditary hemochromatosis causes in adults. But iron accumulation begins much earlier, and symptoms usually appear between the ages of 15 and 30. This disorder is caused by mutations in the hemojuvelin or hepcidin genes.

Neonatal hemochromatosis. In this severe disorder, iron builds up rapidly in the liver of the developing baby in the womb. It is thought to be an autoimmune disease, in which the body attacks itself.

Secondary hemochromatosis. This form of the disease is not inherited and is often referred to as iron overload. People with certain types of anemia or chronic liver disease may need multiple blood transfusions, which can lead to excess iron accumulation.

Risk factors

Factors that increase your risk of hereditary hemochromatosis include:

Having 2 copies of a mutated HFE gene. This is the greatest risk factor for hereditary hemochromatosis.

Family history. If you have a first-degree relative — a parent or sibling — with hemochromatosis, you're more likely to develop the disease.

Ethnicity. People of Northern European descent are more prone to hereditary hemochromatosis than are people of other ethnic backgrounds. Hemochromatosis is less common in people of Black, Hispanic and Asian ancestry.

Your sex. Men are more likely than women to develop signs and symptoms of hemochromatosis at an earlier age. Because women lose iron through menstruation and pregnancy, they tend to store less of the mineral than men do. After menopause or a hysterectomy, the risk for women increases.

Complications

Untreated, hereditary hemochromatosis can lead to a number of complications, especially in your joints and in organs where excess iron tends to be stored — your liver, pancreas and heart. Complications can include:

Liver problems. Cirrhosis — permanent scarring of the liver — is just one of the problems that may occur. Cirrhosis increases your risk of liver cancer and other life-threatening complications.

Diabetes. Damage to the pancreas can lead to diabetes.

Heart problems. Excess iron in your heart affects the heart's ability to circulate enough blood for your body's needs. This is called congestive heart failure. Hemochromatosis can also cause abnormal heart rhythms (arrhythmias).

Reproductive problems. Excess iron can lead to erectile dysfunction (impotence), and loss of sex drive in men and absence of the menstrual cycle in women.

Skin color changes. Deposits of iron in skin cells can make your skin appear bronze or gray in color.

Diagnosis

Hereditary hemochromatosis can be difficult to diagnose. Early symptoms such as stiff joints and fatigue may be due to conditions other than hemochromatosis.

Many people with the disease don't have any signs or symptoms other than elevated levels of iron in their blood. Hemochromatosis may be identified because of abnormal blood tests done for other reasons or from screening of family members of people diagnosed with the disease.

Blood tests

The two key tests to detect iron overload are:

Serum transferrin saturation. This test measures the amount of iron bound to a protein (transferrin) that carries iron in your blood. Transferrin saturation values greater than 45% are considered too high.

Serum ferritin. This test measures the amount of iron stored in your liver. If the results of your serum transferrin saturation test are higher than normal, your doctor will check your serum ferritin.

Because a number of other conditions can also cause elevated ferritin, both blood tests are typically abnormal among people with this disorder and are best performed after you have been fasting. Elevations in one or all of these blood tests for iron can be found in other disorders. You may need to have the tests repeated for the most accurate results.

Additional testing

Your doctor may suggest other tests to confirm the diagnosis and to look for other problems:

Liver function tests. These tests can help identify liver damage.

MRI. An MRI is a fast and noninvasive way to measure the degree of iron overload in your liver.

Testing for gene mutations. Testing your DNA for mutations in the HFE gene is recommended if you have high levels of iron in your blood. If you're considering genetic testing for hemochromatosis, discuss the pros and cons with your doctor or a genetic counselor.

Removing a sample of liver tissue for testing (liver biopsy). If liver damage is suspected, your doctor may have a sample of tissue from your liver removed, using a thin needle. The sample is sent to a laboratory to be checked for the presence of iron as well as for evidence of liver damage, especially scarring or cirrhosis. Risks of biopsy include bruising, bleeding and infection.

Screening healthy people for hemochromatosis

Genetic testing is recommended for all first-degree relatives — parents, siblings and children — of anyone diagnosed with hemochromatosis. If a mutation is found in only one parent, then children do not need to be tested.

Treatment

Blood removal

Doctors can treat hereditary hemochromatosis safely and effectively by removing blood from your body (phlebotomy) on a regular basis, just as if you were donating blood.

The goal of phlebotomy is to reduce your iron levels to normal. The amount of blood removed and how often it's removed depend on your age, your overall health and the severity of iron overload.

Initial treatment schedule. Initially, you may have a pint (about 470 milliliters) of blood taken once or twice a week — usually in a hospital or your doctor's office. While you recline in a chair, a needle is inserted into a vein in your arm. The blood flows from the needle into a tube that's attached to a blood bag.

Maintenance treatment schedule. Once your iron levels have returned to normal, blood can be removed less often, typically every two to three months. Some people may maintain normal iron levels without having any blood taken, and some may need to have blood removed monthly. The schedule depends on how rapidly iron accumulates in your body.

Treating hereditary hemochromatosis can help alleviate symptoms of tiredness, abdominal pain and skin darkening. It can help prevent serious complications such as liver disease, heart disease and diabetes. If you already have one of these conditions, phlebotomy may slow the progression of the disease, and in some cases even reverse it.

Phlebotomy will not reverse cirrhosis or joint pain, but it can slow the progression.

If you have cirrhosis, your doctor may recommend periodic screening for liver cancer. This usually involves an abdominal ultrasound and CT scan.

Chelation for those who can't undergo blood removal

If you can't undergo phlebotomy, because you have anemia, for example, or heart complications, your doctor may recommend a medication to remove excess iron. The medication can be injected into your body, or it can be taken as a pill. The medication binds excess iron, allowing your body to expel iron through your urine or stool in a process that's called chelation (KEE-lay-shun). Chelation is not commonly used in hereditary hemochromatosis.

Lifestyle and home remedies

In addition to therapeutic blood removal, you may further reduce your risk of complications from hemochromatosis if you:

Avoid iron supplements and multivitamins containing iron. These can increase your iron levels even more.

Avoid vitamin C supplements. Vitamin C increases absorption of iron. There's usually no need to restrict vitamin C in your diet, however.

Avoid alcohol. Alcohol greatly increases the risk of liver damage in people with hereditary hemochromatosis. If you have hereditary hemochromatosis and you already have liver disease, avoid alcohol completely.

Avoid eating raw fish and shellfish. People with hereditary hemochromatosis are susceptible to infections, particularly those caused by certain bacteria in raw fish and shellfish.

Additional dietary changes generally aren't required for people receiving blood removal treatment.

Preparing for your appointment

Make an appointment with your primary care doctor if you have any signs or symptoms that worry you. You may be referred to a specialist in digestive diseases (gastroenterologist), or to another specialist, depending on your symptoms. Here's some information to help you get ready for your appointment, and what to expect from your doctor.

What you can do

Be aware of any pre-appointment restrictions. At the time you make the appointment, be sure to ask if there's anything you need to do in advance, such as restrict your diet.

Write down any symptoms you're experiencing, including any that may seem unrelated to the reason for which you scheduled the appointment.

Write down key personal information, including any major stresses or recent life changes. Learn if you have any liver disease in your family by asking your family members, if possible.

Make a list of all medications, vitamins or supplements that you're taking.

Take a family member or friend along to help you remember what's been discussed.

Write down questions to ask your doctor.

Questions to ask your doctor

Some basic questions to ask your doctor include:

What's the most likely cause of my symptoms?

What kinds of tests do I need?

Is my condition temporary or will I always have it?

What treatments are available? And what do you suggest for me?

I have other health conditions. How can I best manage these conditions together?

Are there any restrictions that I need to follow?

Are there any brochures or other printed material that I can take with me? What websites do you recommend?

Don't hesitate to ask other questions during your appointment.

What to expect from your doctor

Be ready to answer questions your doctor may ask:

When did you begin experiencing symptoms?

Have your symptoms been continuous or do they come and go?

How severe are your symptoms?

Does anything seem to improve your symptoms?

What, if anything, appears to worsen your symptoms?

Does anyone in your family have hemochromatosis?

How many alcoholic beverages do you drink in a week?

Are you taking iron supplements or vitamin C?

Do you have a history of viral hepatitis, such as hepatitis C?

Have you required blood transfusions before?

Normally, your intestines absorb just the right amount of iron from the foods you eat. But in hemochromatosis, your body absorbs too much, and it has no way to get rid of it. So, your body stores the excess iron in your joints and in organs like your liver, heart, and pancreas. This damages them. If it's not treated, hemochromatosis can make your organs stop working.

There are two types of this condition -- primary and secondary.

Primary hemochromatosis is hereditary, meaning it runs in families. If you get two of the genes that cause it, one from your mother and one from your father, you'll have a higher risk of getting the disorder.

Secondary hemochromatosis happens because of other conditions you have. These include:

Certain kinds of anemia

Liver disease

Getting a lot of blood transfusions

White people of northern European descent are more likely to get hereditary hemochromatosis. Men are 5 times more likely to get it than women.

Symptoms

Up to half of people who have hemochromatosis don't get any symptoms. In men, symptoms tend to show up between ages 30 and 50. Women often don't show signs of this condition until they're over 50 or past menopause. That may be because they lose iron when they get their periods and give birth.

Symptoms of hemochromatosis include:

Pain in your joints, especially your knuckles

Feeling tired

Unexplained weight loss

Skin that has a bronze or gray color

Pain in your belly

Loss of sex drive

Loss of body hair

Heart flutter

Foggy memory

Sometimes people don't get any symptoms of hemochromatosis until other problems arise. These may include:

Liver problems, including cirrhosis (scarring) of the liver

Diabetes

Abnormal heartbeat

Arthritis

Erectile dysfunction (trouble having an erection)

If you take a lot of vitamin C or eat a lot of foods that contain it, you can make hemochromatosis worse. That's because vitamin C helps your body absorb iron from food.

Diagnosis

It can be tricky for your doctor to diagnose hemochromatosis, because other conditions have the same symptoms. They might want you to get tested if:

You're having symptoms.

You have one of the problems listed above.

A family member has the disorder.

There are some other ways your doctor can figure out if you have it:

Checking your history. They'll ask about your family and if anyone has hemochromatosis or signs of it. They might also ask about things like arthritis and liver disease, which might mean you or someone in your family has hemochromatosis but doesn't know it.

Physical exam. Your doctor will examine your body. This involves using a stethoscope to listen to what's going on inside. They might also tap on different parts of your body.

Blood tests. Two tests can give your doctor a clue about hemochromatosis:

Transferrin saturation. This shows how much iron is stuck to transferrin, a protein that carries iron in your blood.

Serum ferritin. This test measures the amount of ferritin, a protein that stores iron, in your blood.

If either of these shows you have more iron than you should, your doctor might order a third test to see if you have a gene that causes hemochromatosis.

Liver biopsy. Your doctor will take a small piece of your liver. They'll look at it under a microscope to see if there's any liver damage.

MRI. This is a scan that uses magnets and radio waves to take a picture of your organs.

Treatment

If you have primary hemochromatosis, doctors treat it by removing blood from your body on a regular basis. It's a lot like donating blood. Your doctor will insert a needle into a vein in your arm or leg. The blood flows through the needle and into a tube that's attached to a bag.

The goal is to remove some of your blood so that your iron levels return to normal. This could take up to a year or more. Blood removal is divided into two parts: initial treatment and maintenance treatment.

Initial treatment. You'll visit your doctor's office or a hospital once or twice a week to have your blood drawn. You may have up to a pint taken at a time.

Maintenance treatment. Once your blood iron levels have gone back to normal, you'll still have to have to have blood taken, but not as often. It'll be based on how fast iron builds back up in your body.

Hemochromatosis diet

Hemochromatosis causes the body to absorb too much iron from foods. By modifying their diet in specific ways, people with hemochromatosis can minimize the symptoms and reduce the risk of complications.

There are two types of hemochromatosis: primary and secondary. Primary hemochromatosis is genetic, while secondary hemochromatosis can result from health conditions, such as liver disease and anemia.

Most people absorb and lose about 1 milligram (mg) of iron per day. People with hemochromatosis can absorb up to 4 mg of iron each day.

An excessive buildup of iron in the organs can be toxic and cause damage. However, it is possible to maintain healthy iron levels through dietary changes.

In this article, we discuss the foods that a person with hemochromatosis might wish to eat or avoid.

Dietary factors

Spinach and mushrooms are high in nonheme iron, which is unlikely to affect the body's iron levels significantly.

The goal of treating hemochromatosis is to reduce the amount of iron in the body to normal levels.

As well as eating only foods that are low in iron, there are other factors to consider. For example, some dietary components affect how much iron the body absorbs.

Examples include:

Iron type: Heme iron is easier for the body to absorb than nonheme iron. Plant-based foods contain only nonheme iron, whereas meat, poultry, fish, and seafood contain both heme and nonheme iron.

Vitamin C: This vitamin enhancesTrusted Source nonheme iron absorption.

Calcium: This mineral can reduceTrusted Source iron absorption.

Phytates, tannins, and polyphenols: These dietary components limit the absorptionTrusted Source of nonheme iron.

In addition to dietary changes, doctors can treatTrusted Source hemochromatosis with medication and therapeutic phlebotomy, a treatment that removes blood from the body.

There are no formal dietary guidelines for people with hemochromatosis, but some foods that may be beneficial include:

Fruits and vegetables

Fruits and vegetables are an important part of any healthful diet. They are rich in vitamins and minerals that are vital for the body to function properly.

Some fruits and vegetables, including spinach, mushrooms, and olives, are high in nonheme iron. As nonheme iron is harder for the body to absorb, they are unlikely to affect iron levels significantly.

People with hemochromatosis have higher levels of oxidative stress that can be damaging. Eating foods that contain antioxidants can counteract the oxidation and protect the cells from damage.

Many fruits and vegetables are high in antioxidants, such as vitamin E and selenium.

Plants also contain phytochemicals or plant compounds that provide protective properties. Examples of phytochemicals include:

lutein in dark leafy greens

lycopene in tomatoes

anthocyanins in beets and blueberries

Lean protein

Lean protein is an essential part of a healthful, balanced diet, but many sources of lean protein contain iron.

Although there is no need for people with hemochromatosis to avoid animal protein completely, it is best to choose animal proteins that contain lower amounts of iron, such as fish and chicken, over iron-rich animal proteins, such as red meat.

Grains, beans, nuts, and seeds

All grains, legumes, seeds, and nuts contain phytic acid, or phytate, which reduces iron absorption.

Eating foods high in phytates, such as beans, nuts, and whole grains, reduces the absorption of nonheme iron from plant foods. As a result, it may reduce total iron levels in the body.

Tea and coffee

Tea and coffee contain tannins, which are types of polyphenol plant compounds.

The tannins in tea and coffee may reduce iron absorption. Drinking these beverages is another way for people with hemochromatosis to manage their iron levels.

Calcium-rich foods

Calcium can inhibit the absorption of both nonheme and heme iron.

Examples of calcium-rich foods include:

yogurt

milk

cheese

tofu

green leafy vegetables, such as broccoli

Eggs

Research also suggests that eggs can help inhibit iron absorption.

Eggs contain a protein called phosvitin that binds to iron and prevents absorption.

What to avoid

Doctors generally advise people with hemochromatosis to avoid iron-fortified foods and supplements. Other foods to consider avoiding include:

Red meat

Most red meats, including beef, lamb, and venison, are a rich source of heme iron. Chicken and pork contain lower amounts of heme.

As heme iron is easy for the body to absorb, people with hemochromatosis may wish to avoid most red meat.

Red meat also enhances nonheme iron absorption.

Pairing red meat with foods that reduce iron absorption might also help control iron levels.

Raw shellfish

Shellfish, such as mussels, oysters, and clams, sometimes contain Vibrio vulnificus bacteria. These bacteria can cause a serious infection called vibriosis.

People with hemochromatosis are more susceptible to vibriosis infection. Therefore, it is important to cook any shellfish thoroughly to kill the bacteria. People can also reduce their risk of infection by discarding any raw shellfish that have open shells and avoiding eating any shellfish that remain unopened after cooking.

Vitamin C

Vitamin C increases the absorption of nonheme iron. Due to this, people with hemochromatosis should avoid vitamin C supplements.

The amount of vitamin C in fruits and vegetables is generally too low to have a significant effect on iron absorption. These foods also contain a variety of other nutrients that are important in a healthful diet.

However, eating foods or drinking beverages high in vitamin C alongside iron-rich foods may enhance iron absorption. For this reason, pairing iron-rich foods with vitamin C-rich foods may not be the best choice for those with hemochromatosis.

People should speak with a doctor to find out how much vitamin C they should be consuming each day.

Fortified foods

Fortified and enriched foods contain added vitamins and minerals to improve nutrition. Many cereal products are fortified with calcium, vitamin D, and iron.

People with hemochromatosis should avoid iron-fortified foods.

Alcohol

Digesting alcohol causes the body to produce substances that damage the liver.

Combining iron and alcohol can increase oxidative stress. This oxidative stress may worsen the effect of hemochromatosis on the body. Alcohol also increases the body's iron stores.

A doctor may suggest to a person with hemochromatosis that they limit their alcohol intake.

Does diet have much effect on this condition?

Diet can affect iron absorption, but whether it has much of an effect on hemochromatosis is unclear. Dietary changes could be unnecessary in people with hemochromatosis.

According to the American Association for the Study of Liver Diseases and the National Institute of Diabetes and Digestive and Kidney Diseases, dietary changes have only a small effect on iron levels compared with standard treatments for hemochromatosis. Although dietary changes may help reduce iron levels in small amounts, they are not nearly as effective as medications or phlebotomy.

However, the Centers for Disease Control and Prevention (CDC) and the National

Heart, Lung, and Blood Institute still suggest that people with hemochromatosis should avoid:

iron supplements

vitamin C supplements

raw shellfish

high alcohol use

Other treatment options

Treatment for hemochromatosis usually involves:

Phlebotomy

Doctors remove excess iron by drawing about 1 pint of blood at a time. They will regularly order blood tests to check iron levels.

Chelation therapy

Chelation therapy removes iron using pills or injections. These treatments are necessary for people who are unable to undergo blood removal due to conditions such as anemia or heart problems.

Chelation therapies are less effective than phlebotomy in removing iron.

Summary

Hemochromatosis causes people to absorb too much iron from foods.

The goal of treating hemochromatosis is to remove excess iron from the blood through phlebotomy or chelation therapy. Avoiding vitamin C supplements, raw shellfish, and high alcohol use may also be helpful.

Eating foods that are lower in iron or reduce iron absorption may also help keep iron levels within normal limits. However, reducing dietary iron is not as effective as other hemochromatosis treatments.

The Most Important Facts to Know About Diet

Understanding what to eat on a hemochromatosis diet can be incredibly confusing and downright frustrating.

Good information is hard to come by.

Many doctors tell their patients that diet doesn't matter for hemochromatosis, while other physicians recommend overly strict guidelines.

Online resources may provide helpful information; however, they are often generic and don't really teach a person with iron overload to truly understand how to eat healthfully with their condition.

What You Need to Know About Diet & Nutrition in Hemochromatosis

Eating a nutrient-rich, substantive diet helps us to stay strong and healthy.

A frequent response after first hearing a diagnosis of hemochromatosis is to stay away from any iron-rich foods.

It's natural to feel anxious in this situation. If you are concerned with how to eat when facing iron overload, it is common to ask:

How will my life change?

What do I have to give up?

Can I really never eat steak again?

Should I become a vegetarian?

Do I really have to stop eating healthy foods like spinach or oranges?

What can I eat? I'm so confused?!?

When thinking about the best choices for a hemochromatosis diet, you have a lot of options.

Of course, reducing foods high in iron makes a lot of sense, yet it is a rare situation to need to avoid a specific type of food entirely.

Important Considerations to Keep in Mind for a Hemochromatosis Diet

Keep in mind that the severity of your condition will impact how much these "strict" restrictions matter.

Your level of iron overload will determine if you need to watch every milligram of iron or if you can be more generalized in your dietary approach.

The greater your level of iron overload, the more cautious you might want to be with your dietary choices.

The Most Important Foods To Avoid When You Have Hemochromatosis

The most important restrictions in a hemochromatosis diet include:

Avoiding iron supplements

Avoiding raw seafood

Avoiding or strictly reducing alcohol

Iron supplements often contain much higher levels of iron than do foods. Additionally, supplemental iron is usually created for maximal absorption, and that's the last thing we need! Make sure your multivitamin doesn't have added iron, as this is a popular ingredient in women's multivitamins in particular.

Raw seafood and hemochromatosis do not mix. A bacterium called Vibrio vulnificus is present in raw seafood and proliferates in an environment of too much iron. Though very rare, this bacteria has caused severe complications and even death.

Alcohol may compromise the health of our liver, which just so happens to be the most sensitive organ to iron overload. Plus, alcohol has an effect of enhancing iron absorption of food. The combination can be very serious. That being said, some types of alcohol, for some people, in moderation, might be okay to consume. I devoted an entire chapter to this subject in my book, Holistic Help for Hemochromatosis, because this is such a heated subject and of great importance to many people!

Iron-Rich Foods to Limit in Hemochromatosis

Avoiding all iron from food is impossible. Iron is present in foods you may never suspect contain iron, such as fruits and vegetables!

To have a healthy life and a balanced diet, even people with hemochromatosis have to eat iron.

If your symptoms are severe and your health is seriously at risk, being aware of which foods are higher in iron than others becomes important.

If you want a detailed list of the top iron-containing foods in every food group (meat, dairy, vegetables, grains, legumes, etc.) I highly recommend you check out my wife's book, Cooking for Hemochromatosis. Even if you don't like to cook, the extensive charts, analysis, and discussion of every food you can think of will make her book worth your while!

Understanding the Difference Between Heme and Non-Heme Iron

One important distinction to understand when evaluating the iron content of foods is whether the iron is "heme" or "non-heme."

The way our body absorbs these two types of iron is very different.

Heme iron is found only in meat, poultry, seafood, and fish, so heme iron is the type of iron that comes from animal proteins in our diet.

Heme iron is more easily absorbed and is, therefore, a large source of dietary iron for people both with and without hemochromatosis.

Non-heme iron, by contrast, is found in plant-based foods like grains, beans, vegetables, fruits, nuts, and seeds. But don't make the mistake of assuming it's only in plants. Non-heme iron is also found in animal products such as eggs or milk/dairy. It also comprises more than half the iron contained in animal meat.

Non-heme iron is usually less readily absorbed than heme iron. Because of this, you may have heard that you can more safely eat foods with non-heme iron and not worry about how it contributes to your iron overload. This may be true in someone without the genetics of hemochromatosis; however, if you have hereditary hemochromatosis, even non-heme iron may cause problems due to the way our bodies absorb iron.

Iron-Fortified Foods and the Dangers for Hemochromatosis Patients

In the 1930s and 1940s, a new understanding of how nutritional deficiencies were related to diseases (such as anemia), as well as the poor nutritional status of the young men enlisting for WWII, led to the recommendation in the United States in the 1940s (and soon elsewhere in the world) to start adding iron and B vitamins to refined flour.

This practice continues to this day. Considered an important public health measure (for example, iron deficiency anemia is a huge global health crisis that especially affects women and children in the developing world), most refined grain is now enriched to replace the missing vitamins and nutrients that were removed during the milling process.

When a grain is enriched, however, instead of the original natural sources of vitamins and minerals, synthetic B vitamins and highly absorbable iron are added back into the flour. What is not added back are the protective fiber and the phytates (more about phytates in a minute.)

For someone with hemochromatosis, this means that the protective iron-blocking mechanisms of the grain (phytates) have been stripped away, but the iron itself has been put back in, often in amounts higher than were in the original grain and in a format that is more absorbable than the naturally occurring iron.

Enrichment of grains is a HUGE problem for the hemochromatosis community. In many countries, enrichment of grains is mandatory or at least the de facto standard. It is, at times, impossible to avoid.

Non-Iron Nutrients That Impact Iron Overload in Hemochromatosis

Up until this point, I've only discussed the role that dietary iron plays in a hemochromatosis diet. But did you know that the other foods you eat at the same time as iron can play just a big a role as the iron itself?!

Just like in our article about the role that nutritional supplements play in hemochromatosis, nutrients can work in different ways to impact how iron is absorbed from the food you eat.

There are two main categories these other nutrients fall under:

Iron Enhancers: Substances that increase the absorption of iron from your food, making the impact of dietary iron potentially worse.

Iron Blockers: Nutrients that stop the iron from being as easily absorbed, resulting in less iron getting into your body.

Top Iron Enhancers: Foods that Make Iron Overload Worse in Hemochromatosis

The following nutrients specifically enhance iron absorption from meals. Whether from food or from a supplement, care should be taken to avoid these nutrients when consuming foods high in iron:

Vitamin C

Beta Carotene

While iron, vitamin C, and beta carotene are all essential nutrients that we cannot function without, a combination of these vitamins and minerals at the same time can have an additive effect on iron absorption.

The timing of when you take these foods is important. Please do your best to get your vitamin C and beta carotene away from iron ingestion to minimize their impact.

Top Iron Blockers: Foods that Limit Iron Absorption in Hemochromatosis

The following nutrients specifically reduce iron absorption from meals.

Whether from food or from a supplement, you may wish to include these health-enhancing and life-saving nutrients in your diet and supplement regimen:

Turmeric

Milk Thistle

Green Tea

Calcium

Polyphenols and Tannins

Phytates

Oxylates

If you have hemochromatosis, be sure to check with your doctor before starting any supplement, diet, or exercise routine.

A Diet Helpful for Hemochromatosis

Recall, hereditary hemochromatosis is a genetic condition of too much iron absorption.

A proper hemochromatosis diet, as a result, is often based upon other nutrient factors that enhance or diminish the uptake of iron by the body.

Certain food and supplement choices can absolutely make a positive impact.

Pay attention to your iron intake, notice the iron blockers and enhancers, and aim for a healthy, delicious, and nutritious diet.

Eliminating all iron, or all vitamin C, or all of any one type of food may backfire and create new health concerns.

Foods that happen to have some iron in them also often have an abundance of health-promoting vitamins, minerals, and macronutrients to help us be healthy and strong.

These foods should be included and not thrown out with the bathwater!

Nourishing our bodies and enjoying our food are just some of the many reasons why a hemochromatosis diet should not be too restrictive.

Invigorating Lemon Iced Tea Recipe

Ingredients

- 5 cups water

- 2 tbsp black tea powder or tea leaves

- 1/2 cup sugar

- 3 tbsp lemon juice

- ice cubes as required

- few lemon slices for garnish optional

Instructions

Steeping Tea

In a pan, pour 5 cups of water. Heat the water on a medium flame and let it come to a boil.

Once the water comes to a boil, switch off the flame and add 2 tablespoons of black tea powder.

Add sugar and mix well.

Let the leaves steep for 4 to 5 minutes. For a lighter tea flavor, you can steep it for 2 to 3 minutes.

After the tea is steeped in hot water, then add 3 tablespoons of lemon juice. Stir with a spoon.

Now strain the lemon tea in a steel or glass jar.

Let the lemon tea cool at room temperature. Later, keep it in the fridge to let it chill.

Making Iced Tea

While serving, add 4 to 5 ice cubes in a glass. You can add less or more as per your preference.

You can also add 1 or 2 lemon slices. This is optional.

Pour the iced tea in the glass.

Garnish it with a lemon slice or a sprig of mint leaves.

Serve the iced tea immediately. Stir the lemon iced tea with a stirrer or a spoon.

Hot Toddy Tea Recipe

Ingredients

- 1 cup water

- 1 teabag preferably, black tea

- 1/2 lemon

- 1 tsp honey

- 1.5 ounce whiskey, brandy, or rum

- 1 stick cinnamon

- 4 cloves

Instructions

Add the spices to the water and bring them to a boil. Let the teabag steep in this spiced water for 5 minutes.

Strain into a saucepan and stir in the honey. Squeeze in the juice from half a lemon.

Pour into cups. Hold a spoon upside down over the mug and pour in the alcohol. Your hot toddy tea is ready!

Acai Juice Recipe

Ingredients

4 tbsp freeze-dried acai berry powder

- 1 cup mixed frozen berries blackberry, blueberry & raspberries

- 1 cup milk almond or dairy

- 1 tbsp chia seeds optional

- Instructions

- Put the frozen mixed berries in a blender and give them a whiz.

- Add the milk, chia seeds (if using), and the acai berry powder. Give it another whiz until everything blends together.

- Your delicious purple acai berry juice is ready!

Classic Falafels: The Vegan, Fried Fritters

Ingredients

- 250 gm chickpeas/garbanzo beans soaked overnight

- 1 cup onion chopped

- 1 cup coriander/cilantro chopped

- 4 cloves garlic

- 1 tbsp tahini

- paprika

- cumin powder

- baking soda

- oil for frying

- 1/2 cup mint optional

Instructions

Prepping for the falafels takes the night, but it is worth the wait. Take dried chickpeas and soak them in lukewarm water overnight with a pinch of baking soda. There is the option of going for canned chickpeas, but we strongly suggest against it. We don't think that the results are close to each other.

Chickpea in a pan with ingredients for cooking falafel, vegetarian healthy dieting.

Leave them for 6-9 hours and you will find that they have softened the next morning. Drain the water.

Start by patting the chickpeas dry. Add these to the blender and blend till you achieve a grainy breakdown of the beans. At this consistency, they will hold their shape while frying but not taste like a nutty paste.

Add this to a food processor with the other ingredients and blend them till they've mixed well. Use cumin, paprika, and salt as per your taste. If you like the sharpness of garlic, feel free to add a couple of cloves more. It blends well when roughly mashed.

With wet hands, bring this mixture together and start molding them into balls. While making each ball, make sure your hands are slightly wet. It helps the mixture hold shape. Also, if you are new to deep-frying or making fritters, stick to making golf ball-sized rounds.

Let these rest for ten minutes, while you prepare your oil for deep-frying.

Take a wok or a deep frying pan. Make sure it is dry. Place on high heat for half a minute.

To this, add your frying oil. Use oil enough to cover the falafels while frying. We recommend a neutral oil, to begin with. Peanut, soybean, or vegetable oils work well, but you can also use your regular oil unless it has a low smoking point.

Let the oil heat. If you are sure your oil is hot enough, here's a test. Carefully drop a pinch of bread or the falafel dough, if leftover, into the pan. If it rises up and starts bubbling, and does not stick to the bottom or settle in, your oil is ready for frying.

Start by carefully dropping the fritters one-by-one in the oil. Ensure you do not drop them from a distance, otherwise, the oil will splatter out. Also, do not get your hand too close to the hot oil.

Do not overcrowd the pan. Once you see the oil around the individual fritters bubble, gently move them around the pan to ensure all sides have faced downwards.

Once the falafel has browned on all sides, take one out. Break it open to see if it has cooked through properly. If not, reduce the flame before you put it in the next batch. If you are not too sure about your frying skills, test this out with a single falafel first.

Once you have fried your falafels, let them rest for a couple of minutes.

Hummus, falafel, salad in a pan with yoghurt and tahini.

Traditional Dolma Recipe

Ingredients

- 2 onions minced

- 4 tbsp tomato paste

- 1/2 cups uncooked rice

- 2 tbsp pine nuts

- 2 tbsp currants

- 1/4 tsp allspice

- 1/4 tsp cumin

- 1/2 cup parsley

- 1/2 cup mint

- 1 tbsp dill chopped

- 1 pound beef or lamb or a combination minced

- 2 tbsp olive oil

- 1 jar grape leaves drained

- salt to taste

- 2 tsp ghee or butter

- 1/4 cup water plus for filling

- For the yogurt sauce

- 1 cup Greek yogurt

- 2-4 garlic minced

- salt to taste

- 1 tsp olive oil

- For the olive oil sauce

- 2/3 cup olive oil

- 4 tbsp lemon juice

- 1 tsp sugar optional

Instructions

To make the stuffing, add all the ingredients

(except the leaves) in a large bowl and mix

thoroughly. Add a quarter cup water as well. Keep this aside.

Ingredients for cooking dolma (minced meat, fresh grape leaves, butter, rice, mint, onion, dill, spices)

Take the leaves out of the can and immerse in hot water. Let them stay in for 10 minutes. Place the leaves in a colander and wash them in cold water to remove the salt.

If the leaves seem too thick and unyielding, you can blanch them further for 10 minutes in hot water.

Lay a leaf, with the shiny side down, atop a board. Cut out the stem. Place about a tablespoon of the stuffing at the base. Fold the overhanging bottom part over it. Fold in the sides of the leaves. Holding the base, start rolling till you have a neat cylindrical parcel of a stuffed leaf.

Dolma stuffing in a clay pot besides grape leaves

Line a deep base pan with thicker or damaged leaves. This is to prevent the dolmas from sticking to the pan.

Now start laying the rolled leaves seam-side down. Arrange the rolled parcels in layers. Dot it with butter or the ghee.

Cover them with water, so that it reaches just the top of the stack of rolled leaves. If the rolled leaves reach only up to the middle of the pan, put a plate over the leaves and then pour in the water so that it reaches above the plate.

Cover the pan and let it cook for at least an hour and a half. After they are cooked, take out the dolmas and arrange them on a platter.

To serve, drizzle the dolmas with the sauce of your choice. You can serve the sauce alongside. For an easy and quick sauce, follow any one of our recipes.

Yogurt sauce

Mix the minced garlic and olive oil with the yogurt and give it a stir. Taste the sauce and add the salt if needed.

Olive oil sauce

In an airtight jar, add the salt and lemon juice. Close the lid and give the jar a quick shake. The sauce is ready. If you are storing the sauce, give the jar a brisk shake before serving.

A plate of dolmas ready to be served.

Piping Hot Turkish Tea Recipe

Ingredients

- 1 tsp Turkish tea or black tea

- 2 cups water plus, extra for filling

- sugar cubes optional

Instructions

Rinse the small pot with warm water. Pour in 1/4th of the water and add the tea leaves.

Fill the lower pot with the rest of the water and place it on the stove with the small pot on top.

Reduce the heat once the water comes to a boil. The steam from the boiling water at the bottom will gently heat the water in the upper pot.

After 5 minutes, gently pour about half the water from the lower pot into the brewing pot. Add more water to the lower one, place the small pot on top, and put it back on the stove.

Bring the water at the lower pot to a boil and reduce the heat. The steam from the simmering water keeps heating the water on top. Brew the tea for 10 to 15 minutes. The tea leaves will settle at the bottom by the end of this period.

When serving, pour out the brewed tea into the tea glasses according to how strong you want it. The normal serving size is a quarter of a glass. Reduce the amount if you like your tea light or increase it to half-a-glass if you want your tea strong.

Water is then added to the brewed tea in the glasses to dilute it. Turkish tea is usually served without milk or sugar. However, you may add a little sugar to sweeten it. Tea is served on small plates.

A cup of Turkish tea served in traditional style with baklava and nuts in the background.

Delicious Homemade Matcha Green Tea Frappuccino

Ingredients

- 2 cups of milk as per your preference

- 4 cups of ice

- 2 tbsp matcha tea powder

- 1 tsp vanilla extract

- 2 tbsp sweetened condensed milk

- 1/4-1/2 tbsp salt optional

- To make Whipped Cream

- 2 tsp of powdered white sugar

- 1/2 cup of heavy cream

Instructions

To make matcha green tea frappuccino, first, let us start by making the whipped cream. In a tall container, whip together heavy cream and powdered white sugar. Use a handheld blender to mix the two. Continue to mix the heavy cream and sugar until you get soft peaks. Once done, set it aside.

Now, in a separate blender add sifted matcha powder, salt, condensed milk, milk (of your choice), ice, and vanilla extract and blend them together till you get a smooth and slushy consistency.

Once done, pour the drink in two glasses and add the whipped cream and sifted matcha powder as a garnish. Remember to re-whisk the whipped cream till it fluffs up before adding it to the drinks. Use a spoon to add a lump of the whipped cream to the drinks. Serve the cold drinks with a straw and enjoy!

Homemade green tea frappe in glass.

Middle Eastern Pita Bread Recipe

Ingredients

- 1 tbsp instant dry yeast or active dry yeast

- 2 1/2 cups warm water

- 1/4 tsp sugar

- 6 cups all-purpose flour

- 1 1/2 tsp salt

- 3 tbsp olive oil

Instructions

In a bowl of a stand mixer, combine yeast, water, sugar, and 3 cups of the flour to form a sponge. Let the sponge rest for 10 minutes. Mix in the salt and 2 tablespoons of olive oil.

Add the remaining 3 cups of flour little at a time until the dough forms into a nice ball. Knead on medium speed for 5 minutes. It should get smooth, shiny, and elastic.

Use the remaining 1 tablespoon of olive oil to grease a large bowl. Roll the dough in the oil, put it in the bowl, cover it with a towel and let it rise for 2 hours.

Preheat an oven to 500℃ with a baking stone. If you don't have one, just put a baking sheet in the middle.

Divide the dough into 12 pieces. Roll it into 8-inch rounds. Let the rounds rise for 20 minutes. Just before cooking, roll each piece out into an 8-inch circle.

Cook it in batches two at a time on the baking stone. They should ideally puff up and brown in 3-5 minutes.

Now, remove them from the oven and wrap them in a clean dish towel and put them in a plastic bag to keep them soft and pliable.

Pita bread on a wooden board.

How To Make Sour Milk

Ingredients

- Sour Milk with Lemon Juice

- 1 cup milk raw or pasteurized

- 1 tbsp lemon juice

- Sour Milk with Vinegar

- 1 cup milk raw or pasteurized

- 1 tbsp vinegar (plain)

Instructions

Sour Milk with Lemon Juice

To make sour milk, first, add lemon juice to the milk and stir it for about 30 seconds.

As soon as you see the milk and the lemon juice blend perfectly, let the milk rest for 5 minutes at room temperature.

When the milk starts curdling, that's when you know your homemade sour milk is ready!

Sour milk in a parrot green mug

Sour Milk with Vinegar

In an alternate way to make sour milk, add vinegar to the milk and stir it for 30 seconds.

Once you see the milk and the vinegar blend perfectly, stop stirring and let the milk rest for 5 minutes at room temperature.

You will notice the milk starts to thicken.

Your sour milk is ready!

Hong Kong Milk Tea

Ingredients

- 1 cup water

- 3 tsp black tea (loose leaf tea)

- 1/3 cup evaporated milk

- 2 tsp sugar (to taste)

Instructions

To make Hong Kong milk tea, add water and loose leaf tea to a pot.

Bring it to a boil and heat it for about 5 minutes.

Thereafter, take it down from the stove where it had been boiling, add evaporated milk to it and bring it to a boil once again.

Strain the tea into the teacup and add sugar to enhance the taste. You can also substitute sugar with stevia, jaggery or brown sugar.

Serve the beverage piping hot and savor the warm, smooth and creamy texture on your palette.

How To Make Golden Syrup At Home

Ingredients

- To Make The Caramel

- 1/4 cup water filtered

- 1 tbsp white sugar

- To Make The Syrup

- 1 cup white sugar

- 2/3 cup boiling water

- 1/2 tsp lemon juice or

- 1/2 tsp white wine vinegar

Instructions

Boil a cup of water in a saucepan or bring a kettle of water to a full boil.

In another saucepan, begin making the caramel base by warming 1/4 cup of sugar with a tablespoon of water on a very low flame.

You will notice that the sugar starts turning brown, and becomes like caramel.

Now, start adding the rest of the sugar into the saucepan.

Immediately, add the boiling water (2/3 cup) to this sugar mixture. The mixture will bubble but do not worry. It will settle down.

Add the vinegar or lemon juice and keep stirring till the mixture comes to a boil.

Let it simmer on a low flame for 40-45 minutes. You may have to stir it once in a while.

Pour the homemade golden syrup into a clean storage container once it is cool. Don't fret if the syrup hardens during the cooking process. It eventually all dissolves to form a lovely caramel-colored liquid. Enjoy your homemade golden syrup!

How To Make Poppy Seed Tea

Ingredients

- 250 g poppy seeds (seeds from pod, unwashed)

- 2-3 cups water (warm)

- 2 tbsp lemon juice

Instructions

To start off with the recipe, first, pour the poppy seeds into a bottle through a funnel to avoid spillage.

A spoonful of poppy seeds and red poppy flowers on a wooden background

Add 2-3 cups of warm water to the bottle. Ensure that it is not boiled.

Close the bottle and shake gently for 2-3 minutes. This will "wash" off the active compounds, effectively infusing the tea. The water should range from a mild yellow to a dark brown, depending on the type of seeds.

Let the tea steep for 15 mins. You may also keep it longer depending on how strong you want the flavor to be.

Strain the tea into a pot using a strainer.

A teacup with a tea strainer and lemon slices in the background

Add lemon juice to the pot and serve hot.

How To Make Peppermint Oil

Ingredients

- 1 cup peppermint leaves (fresh)

- 1 cup olive oil (or grapeseed oil)

Instructions

To make peppermint oil, crush the fresh peppermint leaves with your hands or chop them using a knife. Thereafter, put it in a glass jar.

Fresh peppermint leaves with moisture on it

Pour olive oil over it and mix thoroughly.

Close the lid, shake the jar, and let it steep for about 1-2 weeks. Make sure to shake the jar at least once every day.

Strain the oil using a fine strainer or a cheesecloth in an airtight container.

Use the oil immediately or store it in a cool and dry place for 3-5 months.

How to Make Clove Oil: Easy Steps

Ingredients

- 8-10 pieces cloves

- 1 cup olive oil (extra virgin)

Instructions

Carefully put the clove pieces into a glass jar.

A close up of wooden spoon filled with dried cloves

Pour olive oil into the glass jar and close its lid.

Pouring oil from a bottle in a bowl

Shake the glass jar and let it steep for 1-2 weeks. Every day shake the jar at least once so that the ingredients mix well.

Strain the oil into an airtight container using a fine-mesh strainer or a cheesecloth.

Use the oil immediately or store it in a dark dry place.

How to Make Ayahuasca Tea At Home

Ingredients

• 200 ml vinegar (white vinegar or vinegar apple preferable)

• 160 g mimosa hostilis (shredded or powdered)

• 150 g Banisteriopsis caapi (powder)

• 3 liters water (filtered)

Instructions

Heat the water in a large pot until it is just about to reach boiling and then reduce to medium heat.

Add vinegar and mimosa hostilis to the water and stir thoroughly.

Mimosa hostilis root bark powder in a spoon

Cook this for 3 hours at low-medium heat. Do not boil!

Filter all the liquid using a hand towel or any other cloth. Squeeze as much liquid as possible from the mimosa.

Store the liquid in another pot and then repeat the entire process with fresh water and the same shredded mimosa.

Repeat the process again. It will leave you with 3 pots of mimosa-infused liquid.

Combine all three pots of mimosa water and cook on medium heat. Reduce it to 1.5 liters, and make it more concentrated.

Put the water in the fridge and cool overnight.

Filter the liquid in the morning to remove any excess particulate matter.

Warm the liquid on the stove again, but do not boil.

Add the Banisteriopsis caapi powder and stir for 15-30 minutes on low heat.

Serve the tea in small amounts.

Okra Water Recipe

Ingredients

- 4-5 okra pods medium-sized

- 1 cup water

- salt (optional)

- pepper

Instructions

Take 4-5 medium-sized okra pods and wash it thoroughly.

Cut both ends of the pods, and slice them in half. You can also use a knife and pierce each side of the pods.

A person cutting okra on a wooden board

Now, take a cup filled with water and immerse the pods in it.

Okra pieces in water in a wooden bowl

Keep the pods soaked in water for 8 hours. Note that you can also keep it soaked in water for 24 hours if you prefer to do so.

Next morning, or after 24 hours, release the leftover sap into the water from the okra pods by squeezing it. You can throw the pods away once you do so.

Pour the water into a glass and drink the nutrient-rich beverage. You can also season the drink with salt and pepper, should you find it bland.

Alternatively, to cut down on the time, boil the okra pods instead of keeping them soaked in water overnight. Once boiled, you can blend the slimy okra pods with water. Either, have it warm as a soup, or wait for it to cool down to have it as okra water.

How to Make Orange Lemonade With Mint & Ginger

Ingredients

- 2 cups fresh orange juice

- 1 orange

- 1/4 cup lemon juice

- 2 cups aerated water

- 1 tbsp ginger juice

- 2 tbsp honey

- 8-10 fresh mint leaves

- ice cubes (optional)

Instructions

In a container add orange juice, lemon juice, ginger juice, and honey. Mix well till the honey dissolves.

Thereafter, cut an orange into half and then into thin slices.

To serve, divide the fresh orange slices and mint between 4 glasses. Add ice cubes if desired. Fill the glasses half with a blend of orange and lemon juice. Top it with cold aerated water. Serve cold and enjoy this refreshing drink!

Mixed Berry Salad Recipe

Ingredients

- 1 cup arugula leaves

- 1 cup blackberries

- 1 cup blueberries

- 1 cup raspberries

- 1 cup strawberries

- 1 tbsp lemon zest or juice

- 1 tbsp honey or maple syrup

- a pinch salt

Instructions

To make mixed berry salad, first, wash and pat dry arugula leaves and the berries.

Combine honey, lemon juice, and zest in a small glass and pour over the salad. Enjoy this delicious salad with family and friends.

Roasted Breadfruit Recipe

Ingredients

- 1 mature breadfruit

- 2 tbsp vegetable oil

- 1 tsp salt

- 1 tsp pepper

Instructions

Choose mature breadfruit with brown patches, instead of a bright green and spiky fruit.

Soak the fruit in water for 2-5 minutes to remove sticky latex or dirt present on the skin.

Using a sharp knife, carve out the stem of the fruit. You can coat the knife with oil to make the carving easier.

Cut an "X" at the bottom of the fruit to allow steam to release when it roasts in the oven.

Coat the fruit with vegetable oil and bake it in the oven at 400 degrees Fahrenheit for one hour. Traditionally, it is cooked over charcoal.

Whole breadfruit being roasted on charcoals

Allow the baked fruit to cool and peel off the skin with a knife.

Cut it into half and remove the core pieces.

Cut the roasted breadfruit into wedges and season it with salt and pepper. Enjoy!

How To Cook Shirataki Noodles

Ingredients

- 1 pack shirataki noodles

- water

Instructions

Shirataki noodles are usually available in packages with water in them. This water smells fishy because it has absorbed the odor of the yam plant. So you need to rinse the noodles very well.

First, throw away the water and place the noodles in a sieve. Rinse the noodles well under running water.

Boil water in a large pot and add the noodles. Cook for 2-3 minutes. This helps remove the bitterness.

Drain the noodles completely. Heat a frying pan and warm the noodles on moderate to high heat; do not add any oil or liquid. This step is important to dry out the noodles completely so that it has a noodle-like texture. This may take 8-10 minutes and it is best done with tongs.

You can now add the noodles to a stir-fry, salad, or make a wonderful warming bowl of soup. Add your choice of meat, vegetables, hot broth, and condiments like miso, red chili paste, or soy sauce. Enjoy!

The Best Coconut Flour Recipe

Ingredients

- 200 grams chopped or shredded coconut meat

- 1 unit muslin cloth

- 1.5 cups of hot water

Instructions

To make the coconut flour, in a blender or a food processor, blend coconut meat and water for a minute at least.

Now take a big bowl and put the mixture in it. Place a muslin cloth over it. Use the cloth to drain the mixture and squeeze out the liquid. If you're wondering what the liquid is, it is nothing else but coconut milk. Keep it aside as you can use this as a substitute for regular cow milk if you're vegan. You can also add it as an ingredient to your desserts, soups, and pasta.

Meanwhile, squeeze as much water as you can, and the remnant inside the cloth is moist coconut flour.

Given that the flour has a lot of moisture in it, take a parchment paper and spread the flour over it in a thin layer. Bake it at 300 degrees Fahrenheit for around 18 minutes.

If you don't have an oven, you can feel free to use a skillet on a low flame. Spread the flour in it and keep stirring it till all the water has evaporated. Ensure that the flour doesn't turn brown. If the flour turns brown, it means that it has burnt and burnt flour is of no use.

Once done, keep the flour for drying. If after drying, you still find it coarse, grind it more till it forms a fine texture. To get a very fine mixture of the coconut flour, you need a powerful grinder or food processor.

This flour can be stored for 3 weeks in an airtight container. It, however, needs to be refrigerated.

Stuffed Summer Squash

- Ingredients

- 2 summer squash

- 4 oz Italian sausage

- 1 garlic clove minced

- 1/2 cup red onion chopped

- 1/2 cup tomato chopped

- 1.5 cups shredded cheese

- 1 tbsp Parmesan cheese grated

- 1 tbsp olive oil

- 1 tsp Italian seasoning

- 1/2 tsp black pepper crushed

- salt to taste

- 2 tbsp parsley chopped (optional)

Instructions

Bring a large pot of water to boil. Cut the squash lengthwise into two halves and scoop out the flesh with a spoon. Keep the scooped out squash aside to use later. Using a wooden spoon, put the squash gently into the boiling water and let it cook for a couple of minutes.

Then, in a skillet, add olive oil and warm it. Add the garlic and onion and stir till softened. Next, add the tomatoes and scooped out squash. Sauté for ten minutes. You can now add the Italian sausage and cook it till brown. Add salt, pepper, and the Italian seasoning.

Preheat the oven to 350°F. Grease a 13 x 9 baking dish with olive oil or cooking spray.

Place the squash skin down in the baking dish. Spoon the sausage mixture into the squash boats evenly. Top them with the shredded cheese and sprinkle Parmesan cheese. Bake for 30-35 minutes till the cheese melts and the squash is fork-tender.

Sprinkle parsley on top, if desired. Enjoy this summer special!

Fried Potatoes & Ramps Recipe

Ingredients

- 4 medium potatoes

- 1 pound ramps

- 1 tbsp olive oil

- salt and pepper to taste

Instructions

Rinse the ramps thoroughly under running water. Remove the hairy part on top of the bulbs and the translucent skin, which is the outer layer of the stalk. Slice the ramps thinly, keeping the green leaves and the white portion separate.

Young green wild onion plants called ramps in hand

Cut the potatoes thin into round slices. In a frying pan, warm olive oil and put the potatoes in. Stir-fry for ten minutes on medium heat and cook till fork tender.

Add the ramps and stir-fry for two minutes. Add salt and pepper to taste. Enjoy this simple and flavorful dish!

French Onion Soup

Ingredients

- 5 onions sliced

- 2 garlic cloves finely chopped

- 2 bay leaves

- 2 thyme sprigs fresh

- 1/2 cup butter unsalted

- Kosher salt

- black pepper freshly ground

- 1 cup red wine or half a bottle

- 3 tbsp all-purpose flour

- 8 cups beef broth

- 1 baguette sliced

- 1/2 pound Gruyere cheese grated

Instructions

First, you take the butter and put it in a large pot over medium flame. Add the chopped onions in it and stir so that the onions are properly caramelized by butter. Once you have covered the onions in butter properly, add garlic, thyme, bay leaves, and salt and pepper to the pot and let it all cook till the onions become translucent or slightly brownish. This would take you around 15 to 20 minutes.

Easy french onion soup ingredients on wood cutting board and wood background, French onion soup ingredients

Next, you add wine to your onions and bring it to a boil, after which put it on low flame till you see the wine evaporate and onions dry.

Now, carefully remove the bay leaves and thyme sprigs from the pot and dust the onions with some flour. Make sure that it is on low flame so that the flour doesn't start to burn. You can also keep stirring the whole mix for the raw flour to cook well without getting burnt.

French onion soup on the black background with its ingredients

Finally, add beef broth and let the soup simmer for 10 minutes. Season it with salt and pepper as per your taste.

All you need to do now is preheat the broiler when you're ready to eat it. Lay down the baguette slices on a baking sheet and cover them with the Gruyere cheese. Let it broil for 3 to 5 minutes until it turns bubbly and golden brown.

Your soup is all set to be eaten now - just serve it in bowls and top it off with several or as many pieces of Gruyere croutons as you want. Alternatively, you can also serve the French onion soup with 2 slices of bread layered with cheese, melted and toasted in an oven.

A Simple Glazed Carrot Recipe

Ingredients

- 1.5 lbs carrots peeled and cut into 1/2 inch thick slices

- 2 tbsp honey

- 1/4 cup butter

- 1 tbsp chopped parsley

- 1/4 tsp salt

Instructions

To make glazed carrots, peel & cut carrots in medium coin-like sizes. Place them in a large pan. Add 1.5 cups of water & bring them to a simmer.

A woman cutting carrots for the glazed carrot recipe

Allow them to cook for not less than 10 minutes or until you feel the carrots are tender. At this point, drain off any excess water.

Once that is done, add the butter, honey, and salt to the pan. Properly stir the carrots along with the honey and salt mixture. Continue to do so until all the carrots are properly coated.

Now let the carrots cook for an additional 4-5 minutes, occasionally stirring it. Stop once the sauce has formed. Lastly, sprinkle parsley or any other herb of your choice over it and serve.

Oatmeal Deluxe

Ingredients

1/2 c. cooked oatmeal

1/2 med. Granny Smith apple

1 scp. Spring of Life Plant-Based Protein Powder, vanilla

1 tbsp. raisins

1/2 tsp. cinnamon

1 tsp. honey, raw

1/2 c. homemade coconut milk

Directions

Dice up half a Granny Smith apple and combine with raisins, cinnamon, honey, coconut milk, and protein powder into cooked oatmeal. Add chopped walnuts (optional).

Spinach, Egg, and Quinoa Breakfast

Ingredients

1/2 c. baby spinach

1/2 c. cooked quinoa

garlic to taste

sea salt & black pepper to taste

2 egg

2 tsp. coconut oil

Directions

Heat 1 teaspoon coconut oil in pan. Add spinach, cooked quinoa, and minced garlic to the pan. Season with salt and pepper, and fry until spinach is wilted. Set aside.

Heat 1 teaspoon coconut oil in pan. Add eggs to the pan, and fry however you like them.

Serve eggs over spinach-quinoa-garlic mix. Top with scallions (optional) and enjoy!

Sweet Potato Hash

Ingredients

1 lbs. sweet potato

1/2 med. onion

1/2 med. red bell pepper

12 oz. canned black-eyed peas

1 garlic

2 tbsp. jalapeno pepper

2 tbsp. cilantro

1/4 tsp. dried thyme

1/4 tsp. sea salt

1/4 tsp. black pepper

Directions

Place peeled and diced sweet potatoes in a large pot. Fill with enough cold water to cover potatoes.

Bring water to a boil, reduce heat to a simmer, and cook potatoes until soft, about 15 to 20 minutes.

Drain and cool potatoes.

In a large bowl, combine the cooled potatoes, sliced onions, diced red pepper, black-eyed peas, chopped garlic, diced jalapenos, cilantro, and thyme. Season with salt and pepper to taste.

Serve cold.

Banana Bread Muffins

Ingredients

3 banana

2 egg

1 1/4 c. oat flour

1 tsp. baking soda

1/2 c. honey, raw

1/2 c. butter

Directions

Preheat oven to 350ºF. Line a muffin tin with paper liners.

Mash the bananas in a bowl. Add eggs, raw honey, and melted butter; mix until combined well. In another bowl, mix flour with baking soda. Combine wet and dry ingredients, mix well, until you have a smooth batter.

Fill muffin cups about 3/4 full of batter. Place in the oven, and bake for 20-25 minutes. Check if done with a toothpick inserted in the center of a muffin. If it comes out clean, they are done.

If you want to make a banana bread, use the same ingredients, but pour the batter into a greased loaf pan, and bake at 350ºF for 1 hour. You can check the center if they're done at the 50 minute mark, but I find that it needs the full hour.

Hit The Spot Hot Chocolate

Ingredients

2 c. almond milk

3 tsp. cacao powder

liquid stevia to taste

Directions

Pour the almond milk into a medium saucepan. Add cacao powder and stevia. With heat on medium to medium-high, stir constantly with a wire whisk until cacao powder is completely dissolved into milk and the drink reaches boiling point. Immediately remove from heat and pour into a mug. Enjoy!

Toasted Almond Smoothie

Ingredients

5 ice

1/2 c. almond milk

1/2 c. canned coconut milk

1 scp. Spring of Life Plant-Based Protein Powder, chocolate

1 tbsp. almond butter

1/2 med. banana

1/4 coconut flakes

1/2 tsp. vanilla extract

1 tsp. coconut oil

Directions

Put all ingredients into a blender with 5 ice cubes and blend until smooth. Really yummy

Spelt Pancakes

Ingredients

1 egg

1 c. canned coconut milk

2 tbsp. coconut oil

1 c. spelt flour

1/2 tsp. sea salt

2 tbsp. baking powder

2 tbsp. coconut sugar

Directions

Combine egg, milk, and oil. Add sifted dry ingredients. Beat until smooth. Bake on hot griddle. Makes 8-5 inch pancakes (give or take).

Healthiest Pancakes Ever

Ingredients

1/2 c. milk, raw or organic

1 1/2 c. old-fashioned oats

1 tsp. sea salt

4 dsh. cinnamon

2 tbsp. ground flax seeds

1/4 c. spelt flour

2 tsp. baking powder

3 tbsp. honey, raw

2 egg

3 tbsp. butter

Directions

Preheat griddle to 300°F.

Combine eggs, melted butter, milk, and honey in a small bowl.

Combine oats, salt, cinnamon, ground flax seeds, spelt flour, and baking powder in a separate medium bowl.

Add the wet mixture into the dry. Mix well.

Pour the batter onto griddle by 1/4 cups. Cook until bubbles begin to pop on the sides. Flip. Cook until sides are more dry. Serve.

Top with strawberries and raspberries, sliced banana, maple syrup, raw honey and/or butter. Serve with bacon (no nitrates or nitrites added) on the side. :)

Homemade Greek Yogurt

Ingredients

8 c. milk, raw or organic

4 tbsp. Greek yogurt

Directions

In a heavy-bottomed pot over medium heat, bring milk to 180ºF, stirring regularly to prevent scorching. Once milk has reached temperature, allow it to cool to 110ºF.

When milk has cooled, add yogurt to the pot and whisk thoroughly to combine.

Pour milk and starter mixture into 2 quart-sized jars (and smaller 1/2 pint to make starter for next batch) and screw on lids. Place them in small insulated cooler and fill with 120ºF water until jars are submerged nearly up to their lids. Put smaller jar on upside down pint jar or something to make as tall as quart jars. Close cooler and leave in a draft-free, undisturbed place for 6 hours or until desired tartness is achieved.

When incubation is complete, remove jars from water bath and place in refrigerator for at least six hours to halt culturing and set yogurt.

The yogurt now needs to be strained. Place a fine mesh strainer over a bowl and line it with 2 layers of cheese cloth. Spoon yogurt into lined strainer and allow to drain for 2 hours or until desired thickness is achieved.

Transfer yogurt to a storage container and refrigerate until needed. Remaining leftover whey (approximately 2 cups) may be reserved for another use if desired.

Homestyle Turkey Sausage

Ingredients

1 1/2 tsp. ground coriander

1 tsp. paprika

1 tsp. garlic powder

1 tsp. sea salt

1/4 tsp. dried sage

1/4 tsp. dried thyme

1/4 c. chicken broth

1 tbsp. coconut oil

1 lbs. ground turkey

2 slc. sprouted whole grain bread

1/2 med. onion

1/4 tsp. cayenne pepper

1/2 tsp. ground cumin

Directions

Finely chop onion in a food processor. Add
all the spices to the chopped onion. Add

sprouted grain bread and chop again in the food processor. Remove the onion/bread/spice mixture and place in mixing bowl. Add chicken broth. Mix chicken broth into onion/bread/spice mixture. Add ground turkey and mix by hand. Marinate for about an hour or overnight. Wet fingers lightly and roll into small balls. In a small frying pan, brown on both sides in coconut oil until cooked through.

Peanut Butter Banana Protein Shake

Ingredients

ice to taste

1 tbsp. peanut butter, creamy

1 med. banana

1 scp. Spring of Life Plant-Based Protein Powder, chocolate

1/2 c. almond milk

1 dsh. cinnamon

Directions

Combine all ingredients in a blender, and blend until smooth.

Clean French Toast

Ingredients

4 slc. sprouted whole grain bread

2 lrg. egg

1/4 c. milk, raw or organic

1 tbsp. coconut sugar

1 tsp. seasoning, Chinese 5 Spice, powdered, organic

1 tsp. vanilla extract

1 tsp. cinnamon

1 tbsp. coconut oil

Directions

Mix together coconut sugar, cinnamon, and vanilla in a bowl (add Chinese 5 spice powder if you want).

In a separate bowl, beat together egg and milk. Add coconut sugar mixture to the bowl, and stir to combine it all.

Soak bread slices to your desired level of moisture - more well soaked makes it almost like bread pudding when cooked.

Spread 1 tablespoon of coconut oil in a pan and cook the french toast for a total of 3 minutes on each side, flipping after 1 minute.

Serve with butter and maple syrup. Garnish with strawberries, blueberries, and/or blackberries. This is a sweet french toast so you can eat it just plain as well.

Breakfast Bars

Ingredients

1/2 c. honey, raw

1 egg

1/2 c. peanut butter, creamy

2 tsp. vanilla extract

2 tsp. cinnamon

1/2 c. walnuts

1/2 c. almonds

1/2 c. sunflower seeds

1 c. shredded coconut

1 tbsp. canned coconut milk

1/2 c. raisins

1/2 c. dried cranberries

2 c. old-fashioned oats

1 3/4 c. brown rice flour

1 tsp. baking soda

1 med. red apple

Directions

Chop the walnuts and almonds. Place all of the ingredients into a large mixing bowl of electric mixer. Using paddle attachment, mix until well blended, about 2-3 minutes.

Grease a 9" x 13" pan with coconut oil. Scoop mixture into pan, and press down evenly. You can use your hands or the back of a spatula.

Bake at 350ºF for 22-25 minutes. (Bars will be soft to the touch when you take them out.) Remove from oven.

Immediately score bars with sharp knife, being careful not to drag the knife, as it will tear bars. I cut these bars 2 x 6 = 12 bars. Let bars cool completely. Re-score if necessary before removing from pan. I place the bars in snack size plastic bags and freeze them for easy daily access.

Fiesta Scrambled Eggs

Ingredients

2 tsp. coconut oil

1/4 c. onion

1/4 c. green bell pepper

2 egg

sea salt & black pepper to taste

1/4 c. fresh made salsa

Directions

Heat coconut oil in a skillet over medium heat.

Add diced onions and peppers to skillet and saute until tender.

Pour eggs over the mixture in the skillet. Season with salt and pepper.

Continue to cook over medium heat, stirring occasionally, until the eggs are completely set.

Serve topped with salsa.

Slow Cooker Apple and Cinnamon Steel Cut Oats

Ingredients

2 med. red apple

1 tsp. cinnamon

stevia to taste

honey, raw to taste

2 c. steel cut oats

2 c. almond milk

2 c. water

Directions

Peel and slice apples and arrange in the bottom of your slow cooker. Add cinnamon, stevia, and/or honey. Add oats, almond milk and water. DO NOT STIR. Cook on low setting for 8-9 hours. Enjoy!

Homemade Muesli

Ingredients

2 c. raisins

1 c. hazelnuts

1 c. almonds

1 c. dried apricot

2 c. dried apples

1 c. coconut flakes

1 tsp. coconut oil

1 c. sunflower seeds

1/2 c. pumpkin seeds

2 c. oats, whole, dry, organic

2 c. barley flakes

Directions

Heat coconut oil in a pan over medium heat. Add pumpkin seeds and sunflower seeds; cook for about 3 minutes, until golden, tossing the seeds regularly to prevent them from burning.

Mix the toasted seeds with the remaining ingredients and leave to cool. Store in an airtight container.

Enjoy a cup of muesli with almond milk or coconut milk for breakfast.

Indian Beef with Spaghetti Squash

Ingredients

1/2 med. spaghetti squash

1/2 lbs. ground beef

1/2 med. onion

1 clove garlic

1 jalapeno pepper

1/2 tsp. ground ginger

1/4 c. canned coconut milk

1/2 tsp. ground cumin

1/2 tsp. chili powder

1/2 tsp. ground coriander

1/4 tsp. turmeric

3/4 tsp. sea salt

Directions

Cook the spaghetti squash: Cut in half, scoop out the seeds, and place flesh-side down on a baking sheet. Bake at 375ºF for 45 minutes, or until you can easily pierce the skin with a fork. Let cool for about 15 minutes, or until squash is cool enough to handle. Use a fork to scrape out the flesh into spaghetti-like strands.

In a large skillet, cook the ground beef and finely chopped onions until the meat is brown. Mix together all the spices and stir them into the meat. Stir in minced garlic and diced jalapeno. Cook 30 seconds. Add coconut milk and cook 1 minute. Stir in roasted spaghetti squash and cook until heated through.

Italian Sausage Stuffed Portobello Mushrooms

Ingredients

red pepper flakes to taste

4 c. spinach

2 tbsp. fresh basil

2 tbsp. fresh parsley

1 c. mozzarella cheese

2 tsp. avocado oil

sea salt & black pepper to taste

4 portobello mushrooms

1 lbs. Italian turkey sausage

1 tbsp. coconut oil

1 sml. onion

4 clove garlic

1/2 c. tomato sauce

Directions

Preheat oven to 375ºF.

Remove stems from mushrooms, and scrape out brown gills. Brush mushrooms with avocado oil, season with sea salt and pepper, and arrange on a baking sheet.

If necessary, remove sausage from casings. Crumble sausage into a skillet over medium heat and brown, breaking the meat up as it cooks. When sausage is browned, remove from skillet and set aside.

Heat coconut oil in skillet over medium heat. Add diced onion, and sauté for about 2 minutes (onions should be starting to soften). Add minced garlic, and continue cooking until onions start to brown. Add cooked sausage, tomato sauce, and red pepper flakes to the pan. Let simmer for 2-3 minutes. Add chopped spinach to the pan, let it wilt and cook down, stirring so it's evenly distributed through the mixture. Remove pan from heat, and stir in half of the shredded cheese, chopped basil, and chopped parsley.

Carefully stuff the inside of each mushroom with the sausage mixture, and top each mushroom with the remaining shredded mozzarella (should be about 2 tablespoons per mushroom). Bake for 15 minutes, until cheese is melted and mushrooms are tender.

Curried Chicken Salad

Ingredients

2 tbsp. golden raisins

2 tbsp. butter

1/2 lbs. chicken thighs or breast

1/4 c. Greek yogurt

1/2 tsp. lemon juice

1 tsp. curry powder

1/8 tsp. turmeric

sea salt & black pepper to taste

1 stlk. celery

1 green onion

2 tbsp. walnuts

Directions

Heat butter in a pan over medium heat. Add chicken pieces and sauté until browned and cooked through. Set aside.

In a medium bowl, combine Greek yogurt, lemon juice, curry powder, turmeric, sea salt, and pepper. Stir until fully incorporated. Add sliced celery, diced onion, chopped walnuts, and golden raisins; stir to mix well. Add cooked chicken pieces and stir to evenly coat.

This dish can be enjoyed warm or cold. Enjoy as is or serve over a bed of your favorite greens.

Turkey Chili

Ingredients

1 tsp. paprika

1 tsp. ground cumin

1/8 tsp. cayenne pepper

2 c. plum tomatoes

1/2 c. chicken stock

1 bay leaf

2 tsp. butter

16 oz. ground turkey

sea salt & black pepper to taste

1 c. red bell pepper

1 med. onion

2/3 c. celery

1 clove garlic

2 tsp. chili powder

Directions

Prepare the vegetables: Coarsely chop the red bell pepper, onion, and celery. Mince the garlic. Chop the tomatoes.

Heat half of the butter in a 3-quart saucepan over high heat. Add the turkey, and season to taste with the salt and black pepper. Break up the turkey and cook for 4–5 minutes, or until browned. Remove to a bowl and cover to keep warm.

Reduce the heat to low, heat the remaining butter, and cook the red pepper, onion, celery, and garlic for 3–5 minutes, or until vegetables begin to soften. Add the chili powder, paprika, cumin, and cayenne and cook, stirring, for 1 minute. Increase the heat to medium, and add the tomatoes, stock, and bay leaf. Bring to a boil over high heat. Reduce the heat to medium-low, and simmer uncovered for 15 minutes.

Add the browned turkey, and simmer 5 minutes more. Remove and discard the bay leaf before serving.

*Note: This is chili, NOT soup, so there is not a ton of liquid in the final dish. If you want this dish to be more "soup-y," increase the amount of chicken broth or add some water.

Dynomite Sloppy Joes

Ingredients

2 tsp. avocado oil

1/2 med. onion

1/4 c. celery

1 med. green bell pepper

1/2 lbs. ground beef

1 c. tomato sauce

Directions

Dice pepper, onion, and celery. Heat avocado oil in a skillet over medium-high heat. Add diced veggies to the skillet, and cook for about 10 minutes. Add ground beef and brown, breaking it up as it cooks. When beef is fully cooked, add tomato sauce. Let simmer for 15 minutes.

Steak and Pepper Crunch Salad

Ingredients

8 oz. beef tenderloin

sea salt & black pepper to taste

3 c. mixed greens

2 tbsp. balsamic vinegar

2 med. bell pepper, any color

4 tbsp. sliced almonds

Directions

Season beef tenderloin with sea salt and pepper. Grill to desired doneness.

Toss mixed greens with balsamic vinegar in a large bowl. Add chopped peppers, sliced almonds, and grilled beef tenderloin (sliced or cubed); toss to combine. Enjoy as is or toss with Isabel's Famous Salad Dressing.

Coconut Chicken Tenders

Ingredients

1 lbs. chicken breast

1/2 c. shredded coconut

1/4 c. coconut flour

1/4 tsp. sea salt

1/8 tsp. black pepper

2 tbsp. coconut oil

1/8 tsp. garlic powder

1/8 tsp. paprika

1 egg

Directions

Preheat oven to 400ºF. Line a baking sheet with parchment paper.

Cut the chicken into strips. Mix together shredded coconut, coconut flour, and spices in a shallow bowl. Lightly beat egg in another shallow bowl. Dip one chicken strip at a time in the egg, then dredge in coconut mixture. Set aside.

Heat coconut oil in a skillet over medium-high heat. Place coated chicken strips in the oil and fry until browned on both sides. Transfer the strips to prepared baking sheet and bake for 5-7 minutes, until chicken is cooked through.

Baked Whitefish

Ingredients

4 oz. whitefish

1 tsp. extra virgin olive oil

sea salt & black pepper to taste

1/2 c. grape tomatoes

2 oz. avocado

Directions

Preheat oven to 400°F. Place fish in an oven-safe dish, surrounded by tomatoes. Drizzle with olive oil and sprinkle with sea salt and pepper. Cook for 8-10 minutes.

Toss together halved tomatoes and chopped avocado. Serve over cooked fish.

Melt in Your Mouth Chicken

Ingredients

1/2 lbs. chicken breast

1/4 c. parmesan cheese

1/2 c. Greek yogurt

1/2 tsp. garlic powder

3/4 tsp. sea salt

1/4 tsp. black pepper

Directions

Preheat oven to 375ºF. Line a baking sheet with parchment paper.

Combine grated parmesan cheese, Greek yogurt, and seasonings. Spread mixture over chicken breasts (whole or cut into smaller pieces).

Arrange chicken on baking sheet. Bake for 45 minutes.

Turkey Meatball Cauliflower

Ingredients

1 lbs. ground turkey

1 head cauliflower

2 tsp. garlic powder

sea salt & black pepper to taste

1 tsp. dried oregano

1/2 tsp. red pepper flakes

4 oz. mozzarella cheese

1 c. tomato sauce

Directions

Place the cauliflower florets in a shallow pan. Add water - just enough to cover the cauliflower. Bring to a boil, reduce to a simmer, cover, and let steam for 7-8 minutes.

While cauliflower is steaming, brown the ground turkey, breaking up the meat as it cooks. Season with salt, pepper, and 1 teaspoon of garlic powder.

When the cauliflower is done, drain it, and season with salt, pepper, oregano, red pepper flakes, and remaining garlic powder.

Stir the cauliflower into the ground turkey. Add shredded cheese, and stir to combine and melt. Divide between 4 plates, and top each with tomato sauce.

Broiled Mexican Salmon

Ingredients

1/2 tsp. black pepper

1/4 cilantro, bunch, fresh, organic

1 salmon

1 tomatillos, fresh, organic

1 1/2 tbsp. extra virgin olive oil

1/4 c. lime juice

3 clove garlic

1/2 jalapeno pepper

1/2 tsp. ground cumin

1/2 tsp. sea salt

Directions

Pour olive oil into a small bowl. Add lime juice, minced garlic, diced jalapeno, cumin, sea salt, black pepper, and half of the chopped cilantro. Stir vigorously until everything is combined; set aside for 5 minutes to let the flavors blend.

While the spices are sitting, get out a sheet of aluminum foil and preheat the oven to 400ºF. Rub the spice mixture onto the salmon. Be careful not to be too rough, but use enough powder so that everything gets in there. Place the salmon on the aluminum foil. Slice the tomatillo very thinly and cover the top of the salmon with the slices. On top of this, sprinkle the remaining cilantro. Fold and seal the foil around the salmon, and place the package onto a baking tray to cook. Bake for 20 minutes, then serve.

Pan Baked Salmon

Ingredients

2 lemon

sea salt & black pepper to taste

1 sml. fresh basil

1 hndfl. fennel, bulb, fresh, organic

32 oz. salmon

1 extra virgin olive oil

1 water

1 sweet potato

1 lrg. yellow beans, wax or french, organic

2 hndfl. green peas

4 tbsp. butter

1 coconut oil

Directions

Preheat the oven to 495°F. In a medium pot, bring the water to a boil, add the sweet potato, and cook for 10-12 minutes or until the potato is nearly done. Add the green beans and yellow beans to the pan and cook for another 4 minutes. Drain the sweet potato and beans together in a colander. Put them into an appropriately sized roasting pan and add the peas, the butter, a little drizzle of coconut oil and the zest and juice of the lemons. Season lightly with salt and freshly ground black pepper, and toss together while still warm. Chop up half the basil and half the fennel or dill, and add to the pan. Score the salmon fillets lightly on the skin side. Rub each filet with salt, freshly ground black pepper, and a little olive oil, and stuff the scores with the remaining herbs. Put into the preheated oven and cook for about 10-15 minutes until the salmon is just cooked (don't overcook it) and the veggies are soft. Serve at the table, giving everyone some veggies and potatoes, a nice piece of salmon, and some of the cooking juices from the bottom of the pan, which are likely a ready-made sauce.

Spicy Honey Chicken Thighs

Ingredients

1 tbsp. coconut oil

2 tsp. garlic powder

2 tsp. chili powder

1 tsp. sea salt

1 tsp. ground cumin

1 tsp. paprika

1/2 tsp. cayenne pepper

1 lbs. chicken thigh, skinless

4 tbsp. honey, raw

2 tsp. apple cider vinegar

Directions

Preheat broiler. Grease a broiler pan with coconut oil.

Combine spices in a large bowl. Add chicken to bowl and toss to coat. Place chicken on greased broiler pan. Broil chicken 5 minutes on each side.

Combine honey and apple cider vinegar in a small bowl; mix well.

Remove chicken from oven; brush half of the honey mixture on chicken. Return chicken to oven and broil 1 minute.

Remove chicken from oven and turn over.

Brush with the remaining honey mixture.

Return chicken to oven and broil 1 additional

minute or until chicken is done.

Lemon Garlic Cod

Ingredients

1/2 lbs. cod

sea salt & black pepper to taste

1 tbsp. butter

2 tsp. extra virgin olive oil

2 clove garlic

2 tbsp. lemon juice

2 tbsp. fresh parsley

Directions

Preheat oven to 400°F. Place fish in a baking dish large enough to hold the fish in one layer. Season fish with a little sea salt and black pepper.

Place butter and olive oil in a small skillet. Heat on medium low. Add minced garlic and sauté for 1 minute. Add lemon juice and chopped parsley, then remove from heat. Drizzle garlic mixture over top of fish. Bake for 12-14 minutes until fish flakes easily with a fork.

Zesty Lemon Chicken

Ingredients

1/2 c. almond flour

3/4 tsp. sea salt

1 tsp. paprika

1/2 tsp. black pepper

1 tbsp. coconut oil

1 tbsp. lemon zest

2 tbsp. chicken broth

1/2 lemon

1 lbs. chicken breast

3/4 c. lemon juice

Directions

Combine chicken breasts and lemon juice in a large covered bowl or Ziploc bag. Refrigerate overnight.

The next day, remove chicken and drip dry. Reserve 2 tablespoons of lemon juice for later use.

Combine almond flour, sea salt, paprika, and pepper. Coat chicken evenly with flour mixture.

Heat coconut oil in a skillet over medium high heat. Add coated chicken breasts to the skillet and brown (should take about 5 minutes on each side).

Arrange chicken in a single layer in a large baking dish. Sprinkle with lemon zest. Mix chicken broth with reserved lemon juice and pour around chicken. Place a thin lemon slice on top of each breast. Bake at 350ºF for 25 minutes, until tender.

Tuscan Meatballs

Ingredients

2 clove garlic

1 med. yellow bell pepper

1 1/2 spg. fresh rosemary

1/2 c. red onion

2 egg

1/2 c. almond flour

sea salt & black pepper to taste

3 tbsp. coconut oil

6 oz. tomato sauce

1 c. chicken broth

1 lbs. ground pork

Directions

Combine garlic, yellow pepper, red onion, and fresh rosemary in a food processor; pulse a few times to chop everything up. Move to a medium bowl. Add ground pork, almond flour, eggs, sea salt, and pepper to the bowl. Use a wooden spoon or your hands to mix well. When everything is well combined, form mixture into meatballs.

Heat coconut oil in a large pan over medium heat. Add meatballs to the pan and brown (approximately 5-10 minutes). Add tomato sauce and chicken broth to the pan and cook approximately 20-30 minutes. Add more broth as needed to ensure liquid does not burn.

Italian Fried Chicken Bites

Ingredients

1/3 c. parmesan cheese

3 tbsp. almond flour

3/4 tsp. dried basil

1 dsh. sea salt

1/8 tsp. nutmeg

1 lbs. chicken breast

2 tbsp. extra virgin olive oil

Directions

Combine grated parmesan cheese, almond flour, basil, sea salt, and nutmeg in a small bowl. Fill a second small bowl with water. Cut the chicken into bite-size pieces, and dip in the water, then coat with the dry mixture.

In a skillet, heat the avocado oil over medium heat. Place the chicken in the pan, and cook until chicken is cooked through, and the "breading" starts to turn a golden color. Make sure to stir the chicken so each side gets cooked.

Move chicken pieces to a paper-towel-lined plate to drain. Enjoy

Easy Crockpot Chicken

Ingredients

2 med. carrot

1 stlk. celery

1 clove garlic

1 1/2 c. chicken broth

sea salt & black pepper to taste

1/2 lbs. chicken breast

Directions

Place chicken in crockpot. Add carrots (sliced into rounds), chopped celery, and minced garlic. Season with salt and pepper. Pour chicken broth over chicken. Cook on low for 6-7 hours or high for 3-4 hours.

Easy Lemon Chicken

Ingredients

1 lbs. chicken thighs or breast

1/2 med. onion

1 lemon

1 tbsp. avocado oil

sea salt to taste

black pepper to taste

Directions

Use a skillet that has a cover. Heat the oil in the skillet and saute the sliced onion until browned.

Lay the chicken on top of the cooked onion in the hot pan in one layer. Slice the lemon very thin and remove the seeds. Press the lemon slices into the top of the chicken (be sure to cover the surface.) Sprinkle with salt and pepper. Brown the chicken on one side. Then use a spatula to flip the chicken and lemon slices over. Cover the skillet and cook on medium low until cooked through. Serve the chicken with the lemon and onion mixture on top.

Notes: the cooking time will depend upon the thickness of the chicken. You can dress the recipe up with minced garlic sauteed with the onion, and/or fresh herbs such as dill, thyme, rosemary put on top of the chicken while it cooks.

Asian Stir Fry

Ingredients

8 oz. ground turkey

2 1/2 c. green beans

1 tbsp. fresh ginger

2 clove garlic

1/4 c. chicken stock

1 tbsp. tamari, organic

1/4 c. apple cider vinegar

1 tbsp. butter

1 1/2 c. white onion

Directions

Brown the ground turkey in a pan and set aside.

In a big skillet or wok, melt butter and add smashed garlic cloves and let saute for 1-2 minutes.

Add in veggies and ginger and saute for a few minutes until onion is transparent.

Add chicken stock, tamari sauce and apple cider vinegar and cooked turkey and simmer on med-low heat until most liquid cooks out (about 5-10 min).

Serve and enjoy. Scallions, chives or sesame seeds are great toppers for this dish.

Rosemary Garlic Chicken

Ingredients

1/2 lbs. chicken breast

1 tbsp. butter

2 clove garlic

2 tbsp. fresh rosemary

1 tbsp. lemon juice

sea salt & black pepper to taste

Directions

Preheat oven to 400°F.

Pat chicken dry and place into a 9x13 inch baking dish. Cover the chicken breasts with butter and minced garlic. Sprinkle with chopped rosemary, fresh-squeezed lemon juice, and sea salt and pepper to taste.

Bake for 20 minutes or until the internal temperature reaches 165ºF and juices run clear (baking time will depend on the thickness of your chicken breasts).

Best Ever Burgers

Ingredients

1 lbs. ground beef

1 tbsp. lemon zest

3 tbsp. feta cheese

2 clove garlic

1/2 tsp. sea salt

black pepper to taste

fresh basil to taste

1 egg

1/2 tsp. extra virgin olive oil

Directions

Mix all ingredients together in large bowl.

Form into four patties.

Grill until cooked to your preference.

If you must add a condiment, I suggest homemade tzaziki or raita, made with a Greek yogurt base and organic vegetables.

Roasted Eggplant and Asparagus

Ingredients

1 lrg. eggplant

1 bch. asparagus

3 tbsp. extra virgin olive oil

3 clove garlic

2 tbsp. fresh basil

1/2 tsp. sea salt

black pepper to taste

Directions

Preheat oven to 400°F.

Slice eggplant. Trim asparagus spears and cut in half. Place vegetables in a 13x9-inch roasting pan.

Mix together olive oil, minced garlic, basil, sea salt, and pepper. Pour olive oil and seasoning mix over vegetables and toss until well coated.

Bake in oven for 45 minutes, tossing vegetables occasionally to keep them well-coated and to prevent them from sticking to pan.

*Feel free to add other vegetables to the mix. Sliced onions and bell peppers work well, but most veggies will do.

Spinach and Feta Turkey Burgers

Ingredients

1 lbs. ground turkey

1 egg

1 clove garlic

2 oz. feta cheese

5 oz. frozen spinach

Directions

Combine ground turkey, lightly beaten egg, minced garlic, crumbled feta, and chopped spinach (thawed and squeezed dry) in a bowl and mix well (using hands). Form mixture into 4 patties. Cook on preheated grill or in a skillet on the stove.

These burgers already have so much flavor that there's no need for any extra cheese or a bun.

Beef with Veggies

Ingredients

1 med. zucchini

1 med. carrot

1 clove garlic

1/4 tsp. chili powder

1/4 tsp. black pepper

1/4 tsp. sea salt

1/4 tsp. dried oregano

1 pinch cayenne pepper

1/2 lbs. ground beef

1/2 med. onion

1/2 c. white mushrooms

1/2 c. beef broth

Directions

Brown ground beef with chopped onion in a large skillet over medium-high heat. Add sliced mushrooms, chopped zucchini, chopped carrot, minced garlic, seasonings, and beef broth. Bring to a boil. Reduce heat, cover, and simmer for 10 minutes. Uncover and simmer for 10-15 minutes, until vegetables are tender.

Sheet Pan Italian Chicken Dinner

Ingredients

- 4 boneless, skinless chicken breast (4 oz. each)

- 3 tablespoons extra virgin olive oil

- 1 tablespoon balsamic vinegar

- 1/2 teaspoon garlic powder

- 1/2 teaspoon dried parsley

- 1/4 teaspoon dried basil

- 1/4 teaspoon dried oregano

- 1/2 teaspoon salt

- 1/4 teaspoon black pepper

- 3 cups cherry tomatoes

- 8 ounces fresh mozzarella (small balls such as ciliegine)

- 1/4 cup fresh basil leaves

- cracked black pepper

Directions

1. Preheat the oven to 425°F.

2. Place the chicken breasts between two pieces of plastic wrap or parchment paper,

and roll or pound them to 1/2-inch thickness.

3. Whisk together the olive oil, vinegar, garlic powder, parsley, basil, oregano, salt, and pepper in a small bowl.

Hearty Italian Beef and Vegetable Soup

Ingredients

- 1 medium onion (about 1 1/2 cup chopped)

- 3 garlic cloves

- 2 large carrots

- 2 celery stalks

- 1 pound lean ground beef (95% lean)

- 2 tablespoons tomato paste

- 2 teaspoons Italian seasoning

- 3 cups beef broth

- 1 can fire roasted diced tomatoes (14.5 oz. per can)

- 1 can cannellini beans (15 oz. per can)

- 1/4 crushed red pepper flakes (optional, more if desired)

- 8 ounces Swiss chard (4 cups chopped)

- 1/2 teaspoon salt (or more to taste)

- 1/4 teaspoon pepper (or more to taste)

- 1/2 cup grated Parmesan cheese

Directions

1. Chop onion and garlic. Peel and chop carrots, and chop celery. Set carrots and celery aside.

2. Saute beef and onion in a Dutch oven over medium-high heat, stirring frequently to break up meat, until beef is cooked through and onion is translucent, 6 minutes. Add tomato paste, garlic, and Italian

seasoning and cook, stirring constantly, until fragrant, 45 seconds. (Pro Tip: Use lean ground beef so the soup won't be greasy.)

3. Add broth, tomatoes, carrots, and celery to pot. Rinse and drain cannellini beans and stir them into pot. Bring soup to a simmer over high heat, cover, reduce heat to low, and simmer until vegetables are tender, 15 minutes. Meanwhile, prepare chard.

4. Strip chard leaves from center ribs with your fingers, and reserve ribs for another use. Coarsely chop leaves.

5. Stir chopped chard into soup and simmer, uncovered, until tender, about 5 minutes.

6. Remove soup from heat. Season to taste with salt and pepper. Ladle into bowls and serve with Parmesan. Cooled soup can be refrigerated up to 3 days.

Quick and Easy Italian Meatballs

Ingredients

- 2 pounds 85% lean ground beef

- 2 cloves garlic

- 2 large eggs

- 1/2 cup dried breadcrumbs

- 1 tablespoon Italian seasoning

- 2 ounces grated Parmesan cheese (2 oz. is about 2/3 cup, for meatballs)

- 1 3/4 teaspoons salt

- black pepper (to taste)

- 1 jar marinara sauce (24 oz. per jar)

- grated Parmesan cheese (for serving)

Directions

1. Preheat the oven to 350°F.

2. Line two baking sheets with parchment paper. Set aside.

3. Grate or press the garlic cloves into a large mixing bowl. Add the beef, eggs, breadcrumbs, Italian seasoning, Parmesan cheese, salt, and black pepper. Using clean hands, mix the ingredients until just combined.

4. Divide the meat mixture into 36 balls, about 1 inch in diameter and 1.5 oz. each, and place on the prepared baking sheets.

5. Bake the meatballs on middle rack of oven until cooked through, 16-17 minutes.

6. Check to see that meatballs are done. Remove from oven or add time as needed.

7. Transfer the meatballs to a large pot and pour in the marinara sauce. Set the pot over medium heat and bring to a simmer. Simmer the meatballs in the sauce until heated through, 3-5 minutes.

8. Transfer the meatballs to a serving dish and top with the grated Parmesan cheese, if desired. Serve immediately.

Hearty Italian Beef and Vegetable Soup

Ingredients

- 1 medium onion (about 1 1/2 cup chopped)

- 3 garlic cloves

- 2 large carrots

- 2 celery stalks

- 1 pound lean ground beef (95% lean)

- 2 tablespoons tomato paste

- 2 teaspoons Italian seasoning

- 3 cups beef broth

- 1 can fire roasted diced tomatoes (14.5 oz. per can)

- 1 can cannellini beans (15 oz. per can)

- 1/4 crushed red pepper flakes (optional, more if desired)

- 8 ounces Swiss chard (4 cups chopped)

- 1/2 teaspoon salt (or more to taste)

- 1/4 teaspoon pepper (or more to taste)

- 1/2 cup grated Parmesan cheese

Directions

1. Chop onion and garlic. Peel and chop carrots, and chop celery. Set carrots and celery aside.

2. Saute beef and onion in a Dutch oven over medium-high heat, stirring frequently to break up meat, until beef is cooked through and onion is translucent, 6 minutes. Add tomato paste, garlic, and Italian seasoning and cook, stirring constantly, until fragrant, 45 seconds. (Pro Tip: Use lean ground beef so the soup won't be greasy.)

3. Add broth, tomatoes, carrots, and celery to pot. Rinse and drain cannellini beans and

stir them into pot. Bring soup to a simmer over high heat, cover, reduce heat to low, and simmer until vegetables are tender, 15 minutes. Meanwhile, prepare chard.

4. Strip chard leaves from center ribs with your fingers, and reserve ribs for another use. Coarsely chop leaves.

5. Stir chopped chard into soup and simmer, uncovered, until tender, about 5 minutes.

6. Remove soup from heat. Season to taste with salt and pepper. Ladle into bowls and serve with Parmesan. Cooled soup can be refrigerated up to 3 days.

Easy Beef Lasagna

Ingredients

- nonstick cooking spray (for baking dish and meat sauce)

- 1 pound 85% lean ground beef

- 1/2 teaspoon salt (for meat sauce)

- 1/4 teaspoon black pepper (for meat sauce)

- 1 teaspoon garlic powder (for meat sauce)

- 1 1/2 teaspoons Italian seasoning (for meat sauce)

- 1 jar marinara sauce (24 oz. per jar)

- 16 ounces low-moisture ricotta cheese

- 1/2 cup grated Parmesan cheese (for ricotta mixture)

- 1 large eggs

- 3/4 teaspoon salt (for ricotta mixture)

- 1/2 teaspoon black pepper (for ricotta mixture)

- 1/2 teaspoon garlic powder (for ricotta mixture)

- 1 teaspoon italian seasoning (for ricotta mixture)

- 1 cup shredded mozzarella cheese (for ricotta mixture)

- 1 box no boil lasagna (12 oz. per jar)

- 1 cup shredded mozzarella cheese (for topping)

- 1/4 cup grated Parmesan cheese (for topping)

Directions

1. Preheat the oven to 375°F.

2. Spray a 9x13-inch baking dish with nonstick cooking spray. Set aside.

3. Spray an extra-large skillet generously with nonstick cooking spray, then set over

medium-high heat. Add the ground beef, salt, black pepper, garlic powder, and Italian seasoning to the skillet. Cook the beef, breaking it up with a spatula, until thoroughly browned, 5-6 minutes.

4. Drain the fat from the skillet. Return the skillet to the stove, and reduce heat to medium-low. Pour the marinara sauce over the meat and stir to combine. Cover and simmer for 2-3 minutes. While the sauce simmers, prepare the cheese mixture.

5. Place the ricotta, Parmesan, salt, egg, black pepper, garlic powder, Italian seasoning, and mozzarella cheese in a large

mixing bowl. Stir with a rubber spatula to thoroughly combine.

6. To assemble the lasagna, spoon 1/2 cup of the meat sauce into the baking dish to cover the bottom. Place 3-4 lasagna noodles in a single layer over the sauce. Drop 1/3 of the ricotta mixture by spoonfuls over the noodles, and gently spread it into an even layer. Spoon 1/4 of the remaining meat sauce over the ricotta. Repeat the layering process two more times. Place the last 3-4 lasagna noodles over the top of the dish, and cover with the last 1/4 of the meat sauce. Sprinkle shredded mozzarella and grated

Parmesan cheese in an even layer over the top of the lasagna.

7. Cover the baking dish with a sheet of aluminum foil.

8. Bake the lasagna on middle rack of oven for 40 minutes.

9. Remove the aluminum foil and continue baking until cheese on top is golden brown and dish is bubbling at the edges, about 15 minutes.

10. Check to see that lasagnas done. Remove from oven or add time as needed.

11. Allow the lasagna to rest for 20 minutes before serving.

Crawfish Étouffée

Ingredients

- 4 tablespoons butter

- 4 tablespoons all-purpose flour

- 1/2 cup yellow onion (diced)

- 1/3 cup celery (diced)

- 1/3 cup green bell pepper (diced)

- 1 tablespoon jalapeno (diced)

- 5 cloves garlic (minced, about 3 Tbsp.)

- 2 teaspoons fresh thyme (minced)

- 1 cup fresh tomatoes (diced)

- 3 cups chicken stock (or seafood stock)

- 1/2 teaspoon crab boil (liquid seasoning)

- 3 teaspoons worcestershire sauce

- 1/4 teaspoon cayenne pepper

- 2 teaspoons Creole seasoning

- 1 teaspoon granulated garlic

- 1 1/2 teaspoons kosher salt

- 1 pound crawfish (tails)

- 1/2 lemon (small, juice from)

- 3 dashes hot sauce

- 1 cup green onions (chopped)

- 1/4 cup flat leaf parsley (chopped)

- 2 tablespoons butter (room temperature)

Directions

1. Start by making a roux: In a large, heavy saucepan over medium-high heat, melt the butter and whisk in flour to combine. Cook until the roux is a shade darker than peanut butter and you smell a faint nutty aroma.

2. Add onions and cook for 2 minutes, then add celery, bell pepper, jalapeño, garlic, and thyme. Cook until vegetables are soft, about 3 minutes.

3. Add tomatoes, stock, crab boil, Worcestershire sauce, cayenne pepper, Creole seasoning, granulated garlic, and

kosher salt. Bring to a boil and then reduce the heat to a simmer, and cook uncovered for 20-25 minutes, stirring occasionally.

4. Add crawfish tails, juice of half a lemon, hot sauce, green onions, and parsley and cook for 15 minutes over medium heat, stirring often. Remove from heat and add remaining butter until combined.

Pressure Cooker Moroccan Chicken

INGREDIENTS

- For the Ras el Hanout spice blend (or substitute 2 tablespoons store-bought blend):

- 1 teaspoon paprika

- 1 teaspoon ground ginger

- 1 teaspoon ground cumin

- 1 teaspoon ground coriander

- 1/2 teaspoon ground turmeric

- 1/2 teaspoon ground cinnamon

- 1/2 teaspoon ground allspice

- 1/2 teaspoon kosher salt

- For the Chicken:

- 1 tablespoon olive oil

- 1 red onion, sliced

- 3 cloves garlic, chopped

- 1 cup low sodium chicken broth

- 1 cup pitted green olives (with or without pimentos)

- 1/2 cup raisins

- 1/2 lemon, sliced thinly, seeds removed

- 3 pounds boneless, skinless chicken thighs

- To Serve:

- 1/4 cup chopped cilantro and/or parsley

- Special equipment:

- 6-quart Instant Pot or other pressure cooker

INSTRCUTIONS

1. Make the spice blend: In a small bowl, stir together the spices and salt.

2. Cook the onions, garlic, and spices: Select your pressure cooker's "Sauté" setting and heat the olive oil. Add the onion and garlic and cook until the onions are

softened and the garlic is beginning to brown, about 5 minutes. Stir in the spices and cook for one more minute.

3. Add the remaining ingredients and pressure cook: Pour in the chicken broth and scrape the bottom of the pot release any browned spices. Stir in the olives, raisins, lemon slices, and chicken thighs.

Secure the lid on the pressure cooker and make sure the pressure release valve is set to its "Sealing" position. Select the "Poultry," "Manual" or "Pressure Cook" setting, and set the time to 15 minutes at high pressure.

When the cooking program ends, either perform a quick pressure release by moving the pressure valve to its "Venting" position, or let the pressure release naturally and leave the chicken on your pressure cooker's warming setting until ready to serve.

Pressure Cooker Chicken with Spices add the chicken and olives Pressure Cooker Chicken with Spices release the pressure

4. Serve: Sprinkle the chicken with chopped cilantro and/or parsley, and serve it with rice, couscous, riced cauliflower, or zucchini noodles.

Sheet Pan English Breakfast Recipe

INGREDIENTS

- 1 1/2 pounds pork or chicken sausage (preferably links weighing 6-8 ounces each)

- 1 cup grape tomatoes, halved

- 8 to 10 ounces baby cremini mushrooms, halved

- 3 tablespoons olive oil, divided

- 1 (15-ounce) can pinto beans

- 1 tablespoon packed brown sugar

- 1 tablespoon ketchup

- 1 tablespoon barbecue sauce

- 4 large eggs

- Salt and pepper

- 3 whole sprigs fresh thyme

- Toast, to serve

INSTRCUTIONS

1 Preheat oven to 400°F. Rub sheet pan with 1 tablespoon of olive oil to prevent the food from sticking.

2 Begin cooking the sausage: Arrange sausage links on the sheet pan and cook for 15 minutes.

3. Flip the sausage and add the tomatoes: Remove sheet pan from the oven and using tongs. Add the grape tomatoes, cut side up and season with a pinch of salt and pepper.

Return to oven and bake for another 15 minutes.

Cooking the sausages and tomatoes for British Breakfast on a sheet pan

4. Meanwhile, prep the remaining ingredients. Toss the mushrooms with 1 tablespoon olive oil and a pinch of salt and pepper, and set aside. Drain and rinse pinto beans and stir them together with brown sugar, ketchup, and barbecue sauce. Transfer beans to a small oven-safe skillet or dish.

Cook the beans for a traditional british breakfast in a separate skillet

5. Pour off liquid and add the mushrooms. Remove the sheet pan from the oven (at this point, the sausages have been cooking for 30 minutes and the tomatoes for 15 minutes). If there is a lot of liquid on the sheet pan, carefully pour off the liquid; do not stir the tomatoes (they tend to fall apart if stirred and are better left alone).

Add prepared mushrooms to the sheet pan and return to the oven.

A sheet pan with sausages, tomatoes, and potatoes for a full english breakfast

6. Add the beans and the eggs. After 15 more minutes (40-45 total minutes of baking), remove the sheet pan and again drain off any excess liquid. Flip the sausages again, but the other ingredients can be left alone.

Clear a little space on the sheet pan and nestle the dish of beans inside. (Alternatively, if you're running out of space, you can bake the beans on a separate oven rack.)

Make four little pockets of space on the sheet pan for the eggs. Drizzle a tiny amount of oil in each area and crack in eggs. Place the fresh thyme sprigs here and there over the ingredients.

Eggs cracked on a sheet pan with sausages, tomatoes, potatoes, and a pot of beans

7. Bake the eggs: Bake for a final 5 minutes, just until the whites of the eggs set. (If you want the eggs cooked through with hard yolks, bake them for 8 minutes total.)

While the eggs bake, make the toast.

8. Season and serve: Remove sheet pan from the oven and allow to cool briefly. Sprinkle everything with salt and pepper. Slice sausage and divide between plates. Serve with beans, roasted tomatoes and mushrooms, eggs, and crispy toast.

Sheet Pan Fish and Chips Recipe

INGREDIENTS

• 6 tablespoons olive oil, or more if needed

• 2 1/2 pounds Yukon Gold or other yellow potatoes (3 large or 6 medium), unpeeled

- 1 teaspoon salt

- 1 cup Panko, or other unseasoned dry white breadcrumbs

- 1/2 teaspoon ground black pepper

- 2 pounds firm-fleshed white fish fillets, skins removed, such as haddock, halibut, pollock, flounder, whiting, redfish, cod, or other fish in your region

- 1 tablespoon chopped fresh parsley

- 1 lemon, cut into wedges, to serve

- Tartar sauce, to serve

INSTRCUTIONS

1. Heat the oven to 450F. Arrange 2 oven racks in the top and bottom third of the oven. Line 2 baking sheets with foil and coat with olive oil (about 1 tablespoon per baking sheet) or with nonstick cooking spray.

2. Prepare the potatoes: Quarter the potatoes lengthwise, then cut each quarter in half again so you get 8 spears from each potato. In a bowl, toss the potatoes with 2 tablespoons of the oil and 1/2 teaspoon salt. Spread the potatoes on one of the baking sheets with their wedges pointing up, if possible, so the cut sides are exposed (some may not stand; that's OK).

3. Roast the potatoes: Roast the spears on the lower rack in the oven for 40 minutes. Rotate the pan partway through (after 20 minutes of cooking) and use a wide metal spatula to stir the potatoes. At this point, it's fine if the potatoes fall on their sides; the sides touching the pan will become extra-crispy and golden.

4. Toast the panko: Once the potatoes are in the oven, start on the panko and the fish. To toast the panko, warm a heavy skillet over medium high heat. Add the panko (no oil needed), and lower the heat to medium. Slowly toast the panko, stirring frequently,

for 10 to 15 minutes or until a deep golden brown.

Remove the skillet from heat. Stir 1 tablespoon of olive oil, 1/2 teaspoon salt, and 1/2 teaspoon black pepper into the panko breadcrumbs until they are well coated. Transfer the crumbs to a shallow bowl.

5. Prepare the fish: Cut the fish into large strips ("fingers") or big 3-inch pieces, however you prefer. Rub all the pieces with the remaining tablespoon of olive oil.

6. Coat the fish with panko: Press the fish into the panko so the pieces are coated all over. Set the fish on the second baking sheet, spaced slightly apart.

7. When the potatoes are 15 to 20 minutes away from being done, bake the fish: Cook thick (2-inch) fish fillets for 15 to 18 minutes and thinner (1 1/2-inch or thinner) fillets for 10 to 13 minutes, or until the fish is firm and the coating is starting to brown. Err on the side of caution and do not over-bake.

7. Serve the fish and chips: Arrange fish and potato spears on plates, sprinkle with parsley, serve with lemon and tartar sauce.

Chicken Mulligatawny Soup

INGREDIENTS

- 2 tablespoons butter

- 1 tablespoon extra virgin olive oil

- 1 large onion, chopped (about 2 cups)

- 2 ribs celery, chopped (about 1 cup)

- 2 carrots, chopped (about 1 cup)

- 2 bay leaves

- 4 teaspoon yellow curry powder

- 1 1/4 pound (570 g) boneless, skinless chicken thighs, trimmed of visible fat

- 2 cups (475 ml) chicken stock

- 2 cups (475 ml) water

- 1 1/2 teaspoons kosher salt (or 1 teaspoon sea salt)

- 1/4 cup uncooked basmati rice

- 2 tart apples, cored, peeled, and chopped (about 2 cups)

- 1/4 (60 ml) cup heavy whipping cream

- 1/4 cup (60 ml) plain yogurt for garnish

- 1 tablespoon minced chives for garnish

INSTRCUTIONS

1. Sauté onions, celery, carrots in olive oil and butter, add bay leaves, curry powder: Heat butter and olive oil on medium high heat in a large (4 to 5 quart), thick-bottomed pot. Add the onions, celery, and carrots. Cook for 5 minutes until just starting to soften. Add the bay leaves. Add the curry powder and mix to coat.

2. Add chicken, stock, salt: Add the chicken thighs and stir to coat with the curry mixture. Add the stock and water to the pot. Add the salt. Bring to a simmer and reduce the heat to maintain a simmer. Cover and cook for 20 minutes.

3. Remove chicken, let cool to touch: Remove the chicken pieces from the pot. (They should be just cooked through. If not, return them to the pot for another 5 minutes or so, until they are cooked through.) Place on a cutting board and allow to cool to the touch.

4. Add rice, apples: Add the rice and the chopped apples to the soup. Return to a simmer on high heat, then lower the heat to maintain a low simmer. Cover and cook for 15 minutes, or until the rice is cooked through.

5. Shred the chicken, return to soup, add cream: While the apples and rice are cooking in the soup, shred the chicken, discarding any tough bits. Once the rice and apples in the soup are cooked, add the chicken back to the pot. Heat for 5 minutes more. Then stir in the cream.

Náutica Tropical Smoothie Recipe

INGREDIENTS

1 cup fresh watermelon juice

3 tbs creamed coconut in a can

1 cup frozen pineapple

1/2 cup frozen strawberry

1/2 cup frozen banana

One pouch of Náutica Sea Moss

INSTRUCTIONS

1. Add all liquids first, including Náutica Sea Moss.

2. Blend all frozen fruits and ingredients together until smooth.

3. Sprinkle some chia seeds and shredded coconut on top and garnish however you like!

Black Bean And Mango Salsa

INGREDIENTS

- 1 (14.5) ounce can black beans, drained and rinsed

- 3 ripe mangos, diced

- 1 medium red bell pepper, chopped

- ½ cup chopped red onion

- ¼ cup packed fresh cilantro leaves, chopped

- 1 jalapeño, seeded and minced

- ¼ cup fresh lime juice

- 2 tablespoons olive oil

- 1/2 teaspoon cumin

- ⅛ to ¼ teaspoon salt, to taste

DIRECTIONS

1. Combine everything together in a large bowl. Season to taste, adding more salt or lime juice as desired.

2. Serve with tortilla chips, vegetable scoops or as a side dish.

Chicken Rollatini

INGREDIENTS

Four even-sized, medium chicken breasts

1 tsp garlic powder

2 tsp dried Italian seasonings

8 oz jar sun-dried tomatoes, drained

10 oz jar roasted red peppers, drained

Four cloves fresh or roasted garlic

2 Tbsp. chicken broth

Toothpicks

2 Tbsp. dried or fresh parsley

INSTRUCTIONS

1. Preheat your oven to 375 degrees Fahrenheit.

2. Prepare a baking sheet pan with parchment or cooking spray.

3. Place chicken breasts in between parchment paper or plastic wrap.

4. Gently, and carefully pound chicken breasts into thin/even "pancake-like" 1/2-

inch-thick pieces with a mallet or the bottom of a heavy pan.

5. Season with garlic powder & Italian seasonings and rub seasonings into the meat on all sides.

6. In a blender or food processor, purée 8 oz jar Sun-Dried Tomatoes (drained well), a 10-12 oz jar Red Roasted Peppers (drained well-or roast your own), and your garlic. Add a tiny bit of organic Chicken Broth (or water), if necessary, to create a nice, thick sauce puree.

7. Spread a thin layer of the purée (about 2-3 Tablespoons) onto one side of each

chicken breast, and top this with a sprinkle of dried or fresh Italian parsley.

8. Roll chicken up, encompassing the puree, as shown, using a toothpick to hold each together, and place rolls onto your lightly sprayed flat sheet pan.

9. Bake in your preheated 375 Fahrenheit degree oven for about 30-35 minutes, or just until chicken is cooked through, finishing with a quick (1-2 minutes) broil to brown the tops.

10. Serve with roasted green beans! Consider incorporating some greens: Add a

few pieces of fresh spinach or kale before rolling up the chicken.

Hearty Burrito Bowls

INGREDIENTS

2 cups cooked quinoa, or cooked brown rice

1 (15 oz. can) organic black beans, drained and rinsed

Lime wedges, to garnish

Jalapeno slices to garnish

PICO DE GALLO

2 cups chopped fresh tomatoes

One small white onion, diced

1-2 jalapeños, seeded and chopped

A good handful of fresh cilantro leaves, chopped

Juice and zest of 1 lime

Sea salt and freshly ground black pepper, to your taste

BURRITO MEAT

2 lbs. lean ground turkey or lean ground beef

1 Tbsp olive oil

1 (15 oz. jar) fire-roasted diced tomatoes, with juice

1 cup organic tomato sauce

2 tsp chili powder

2 tsp ground cumin

1/2 tsp ground coriander seed

1 tsp onion powder

1 tsp paprika

Sea salt and pepper to taste, about 1/4 teaspoon each

INSTRUCTIONS

1. Heat a heavy skillet over medium-high heat, and once hot add in your oil. Add in the ground meat and cook, breaking it up with a wooden spoon to evenly brown it, about 6-8 minutes.

2. Once the meat is evenly browned, then drain excess grease.

3. Sprinkle cooked and drained meat with seasonings and stir in your fire-roasted tomatoes, and tomato sauce; cook until its thick and bubbling, about 10 minutes.

4. Once your meat sauce has thickened, remove from the heat and let cool.

5. In a medium to a large glass bowl, gently stir together your Pico de Gallo ingredients, taste test, and adjust as you like.

6. To assemble these beautiful meal prep bowls, evenly divide your cooked quinoa/rice among four glass containers.

7. Arrange the burrito meat equally next to the quinoa, then add beans, corn, and Pico de Gallo as shown.

8. Garnish with thinly sliced jalapeños and lime wedges if desired.

9. Refrigerate for up to 4 days.

Enjoy!

Baked Shrimp Salmon

INGREDIENTS

2 lbs. fresh salmon fillets

1 lb. large shrimp, uncooked

3 Tbsp oil (olive or canola)

1/2 lb. asparagus

One large lemon, sliced

One stick unsalted butter, sliced

SEASONING

1 ½ tsp ground paprika

2 tsp table salt

½ tsp ground black pepper

2 tsp garlic powder

INSTRUCTIONS

1. De-vein shrimp and remove the tail, if desired. Trim ends of asparagus.

2. Preheat oven to 425°F.

3. Combine all ingredients for the seasoning.

4. Cut salmon into four or five equal parts.

5. Arrange salmon and asparagus on a large baking sheet. Season salmon and asparagus (there will be leftover seasoning). Add lemon and butter slices to salmon and the asparagus. Drizzle with oil. Bake 5 minutes.

6. Meanwhile, season shrimp and toss to coat.

7. Add shrimp to the baking sheet, spread out evenly. Add leftover butter and lemon over shrimp. Return to oven. Bake another 7-9 minutes, until shrimp and salmon are fully cooked.

8. Pour the butter juices over the salmon, shrimp, and asparagus.

Enjoy!

Spring Detox Cauliflower Salad

INGREDIENTS

1 14-ounce can chickpeas, drained and rinsed

chili powder, salt, and pepper, to taste

1 head cauliflower, cut into florets

1 apple, sliced thin

1 shallot, sliced thin

a handful of parsley and mint, chopped

2 firm avocados, cut into chunks

DRESSING:

2 tablespoons grainy mustard

2 tablespoons honey

1/4 cup olive oil

1/4 cup water

juice and zest of one lime

salt and pepper, to taste

INSTRUCTIONS

Chickpeas: Preheat oven to 400 degrees. Place chickpeas on a baking sheet lined with parchment. Drizzle with olive oil and sprinkle with chili powder, salt, and pepper to taste. Roast for 20-30 minutes until crispy and browned.

Cauliflower Prep: Working in batches, run the cauliflower florets through a food processor until you get "rice" – it should take about 20-30 pulses.

Dressing: Shake up all the ingredients in a jar or whisk together. Taste and adjust.

Assembly: Toss everything together. That's it!

Detox Chicken Soup

INGREDIENTS

3-4 small chicken breasts

3 Tbsps. avocado oil, coconut, or olive oil, divided

1 large yellow onion, diced small

4-5 large celery stalks, sliced

2 large carrots, peeled and chopped

1 red bell pepper, diced

8 cups organic chicken broth, or bone broth

1/2 tsp. turmeric powder

1½ tsp. sea salt

15 oz cooked chickpeas or white beans, drained and rinsed

2 cups organic broccoli florets, bite-size

INSTRUCTIONS

1. In a large stockpot or Dutch oven, heat 2 Tbsps. oil over medium-high heat and cook chicken breast until nicely browned, about 4 minutes on each side.

2. Set aside on a plate and shred it using 2 forks once cool.

3. Add the remaining oil and sauté onion, celery and carrots, and pepper stirring occasionally, for about 5 minutes.

4. Stir in the chicken stock, turmeric, sea salt, and chickpeas, or white beans; bring to a boil.

5. Add shredded chicken, cover and turn down the heat to a simmer for about 20 minutes.

6. Add broccoli, cover and simmer an additional 8-10 minutes on low. Enjoy!

Philly Cheese Steak Stuffed Bell Peppers

INGREDIENTS

4 bell peppers, halved

1 tbsp. vegetable oil

1 large onion, sliced

16 oz. cremini mushrooms, sliced

Kosher salt

Freshly ground black pepper

1 1/2 lb. sirloin steak, thinly sliced

2 tsp. Italian seasoning

16 slices of provolone cheese

Freshly chopped parsley, for garnish

DIRECTIONS

1. Preheat oven to 325 degrees. Place peppers in a large baking dish and bake until tender, 30 minutes.

2. Meanwhile, in a large skillet over medium-high heat, heat oil. Add onions and mushrooms and season with salt and pepper. Cook until soft, 6 minutes. Add

steak and season with more salt and pepper. Cook, stirring occasionally, 3 minutes. Stir in Italian seasoning.

3. Add provolone to bottom of baked peppers and top with steak mixture. Top with another piece of provolone and broil until golden, 3 minutes.

4. Garnish with parsley before serving.

Enjoy!

Garlic Parmesan Baked Carrot Fries

INGREDIENTS

for 2 servings

2 carrots

1 tablespoon oil

¼ cup parmesan cheese

1 tablespoon garlic powder

1 teaspoon pepper

¼ cup fresh parsley, chopped

½ teaspoon salt

DIPPING SAUCE

2 tablespoons plain Oikos Triple Zero Greek yogurt

1 tablespoon lemon juice

½ teaspoon garlic salt

1 teaspoon pepper

PREPARATION:

1. Preheat oven to 400°F (200°C).

2. Slice the top and bottom off of carrots then slice them in half, slice each half into thirds lengthwise.

3. In a large bowl, mix ingredients with carrot sticks.

4. Spread on a baking sheet.

5. Bake for 15-20 minutes (depending on how crispy you want them).

6. Mix together ingredients for dipping sauce in a small bowl.

7. Serve warm carrots with dipping sauce. Topped with Parmesan and parsley.

Spice-Roasted Salmon With Roasted Cauliflower

Ingredients:

1 tablespoon olive oil

1 teaspoon ground cumin, divided

3/4 teaspoon kosher salt, divided

1/8 teaspoon freshly ground black pepper

4 cups cauliflower florets

1/4 cup chopped fresh cilantro

1 tablespoon fresh lemon juice

1/2 teaspoon ground coriander

1/8 teaspoon ground allspice

4 (4 1/2-oz.) skin-on salmon fillets (about 1 in. thick)

Cooking spray

4 lemon wedges

1. Preheat oven to 450°F.

2. Combine olive oil, 1/2 teaspoon ground cumin, 1/4 teaspoon salt, and black pepper in a large bowl. Add cauliflower florets; toss well to coat.

3. Arrange cauliflower in a single layer on a rimmed baking sheet; bake at 450°F for 18 to 20 minutes or until cauliflower is browned

and tender. Combine the cauliflower mixture, cilantro, and lemon juice in a bowl; toss gently to combine.

4. Reduce oven temperature to 400°F.

5. Combine remaining 1/2 teaspoon cumin, remaining 1/2 teaspoon salt, coriander, and allspice in a small bowl. Rub spice mixture evenly over fillets.

6. Arrange fillets, skin side down, on a foil-lined baking sheet coated with cooking spray; bake at 400°F for 10 minutes or until done. Serve with cauliflower mixture and lemon wedges.

Greek Salad Wraps

Ingredients:

⅓ cup red-wine vinegar

¼ cup extra-virgin olive oil

2 tablespoons finely chopped fresh oregano

¼ teaspoon salt

¼ teaspoon ground pepper

8 cups chopped romaine lettuce

1 (15 ounce) can reduced-sodium chickpeas, rinsed

1 medium cucumber, halved and sliced (1½ cups)

1 cup halved cherry or grape tomatoes

¼ cup sliced pitted Kalamata olives

¼ cup slivered red onion

6 8- or 9-inch tortillas (like Ezekiel sprouted whole grain tortillas)

Directions

1. Whisk vinegar, oil, oregano, salt and pepper in a large bowl.

2. Add romaine, chickpeas, cucumber, tomatoes, olives, and onion; toss to coat.

3. Place about 1½ cups of the salad on each wrap and roll into a wrap sandwich.

Slim AM Jello Pops

Ingredients:

- 1 cup of hot water

- 1 packet of raspberry jello

- 1 sachet Slim Am

- 1 cup of cold water

Directions:

1. Bring to a boil 1 cup of water.

2. Pour the boiled water into a bowl.

3. Add 1 packet of raspberry Jello and Slim Am powder.

4. Stir until dissolved.

5. Add 1 cup of cold water and continue to stir.

6. Pour into mini cups and insert popsicle sticks.

7. Refrigerate for 4-8 hours.

Watermelon Pizza

Ingredients:

• 1 Cup of non-fat Greek yogurt

• ½ Scoop Slim Am Raspberry Flavor

• Triangle sliced watermelon

Directions:

1. In a large bowl, mix in the yogurt, Slim Am and mix.

2. Spread the yogurt mix on the watermelon slices.

3. Add fruit of choice for toppings.

Acai AM Bowl

Ingredients:

- 12 oz. Plain non-fat yogurt

- 2 Tbsp Acai berry blend

- 1 Scoop Slim AM Raspberry Flavor

- Preferred fruit (blueberries, strawberries & banana)

- Granola

- Honey (optional)

- Shredded coconut (optional)

Directions:

1. In a large bowl add the nonfat yogurt, acai berry blend, Slim Am and mix thoroughly.

2. Add in fruit of choice, granola and a drizzle of honey

Poached Egg On Avocado Toast

Ingredients:

1 slice bread (such as Ezekiel bread)

1/2 avocado

One egg

Lemon juice

Salt and pepper to taste

Cayenne pepper

Directions

1. Start by poaching an egg.

2. Toast one piece of Ezekiel bread (80 calories)

3. Slice ½ cup of avocado (117 calories) and smash in a bowl. Add a dash of lemon juice, salt and pepper.

4. Spoon onto toasted bread and, if desired, top with red pepper flakes to add a little kick.

5. Top with your poached egg and enjoy!

Spring Salad with Slim AM dressing

Ingredients:

¼ Cup raspberries (fresh)

2 Tbsp water

2 Tbsp olive oil

1 Tbsp apple cider vinegar

Pinch of salt & pepper

1 Satchet Slim Am Raspberry

2 Cups of Spinach

4 sliced strawberries

5-7 grape tomatoes

3-4 Slices of orange peppers

¼ Cup of pecans

¼ Cup Feta cheese

Directions:

1. In a blender, add raspberries, water, olive oil, apple cider vinegar, salt & pepper, and Slim Am.

2. Blend

3. On a large plate, prepare desired salad bed with toppings.

4. Add Slim Am dressing.

Roasted Red Pepper Mozzarella And Basil Stuffed Chicken

Ingredients:

4 chicken breasts boneless and skinless

8 ounces fresh mozzarella cheese; sliced into 8 slices

1 12 oz jar roasted red peppers; sliced into 1-inch pieces

1 bunch basil fresh; whole leaves

1/4 cup parmesan cheese grated

1 tablespoon Italian seasoning

Salt & pepper; for seasoning

Directions

1. Preheat oven to 400 degrees. Grease a 9 x 12 casserole dish. Butterfly chicken breasts by slicing into the long side of the breast, stopping just about 1/4 of an inch from the opposite side. Lay chicken breast in casserole dish opened up.

2. Sprinkle the exposed insides of the chicken breast with 1/2 of the Italian seasoning and salt and pepper. Stack the roasted red pepper, basil, and 1 slice of the mozzarella on the bottom side of the chicken. Fold the top flap of the chicken over, tucking in the mozzarella, basil and

roasted red pepper as necessary. Sprinkle with the remaining Italian seasoning.

3. Bake chicken for 30-40 minutes (until chicken is no longer pink). Pull chicken out of oven and turn the oven to a high broil. Top chicken with remaining mozzarella slices and sprinkle with Parmesan cheese. Broil until cheese is browned and bubbly, about 5 minutes.

Veggie And Hummus Sandwich

Ingredients:

2 slices bread (such as Ezekiel bread)

3 tablespoons hummus

¼ avocado, mashed

½ cup mixed salad greens

¼ medium red bell pepper, sliced

¼ cup sliced cucumber

¼ cup shredded carrot

Directions

1. Spread one slice of bread with hummus and the other with avocado.

2. Fill the sandwich with greens, bell pepper, cucumber, and carrot. Slice in half and serve.

Salmon Salad-Stuffed Avocado

Ingredients:

⅓ cup canned salmon

1 tablespoon pesto

1 tablespoon nonfat plain Greek yogurt (such as Oikos Triple Zero)

2 teaspoons minced shallot

½ avocado

1 cup baby spinach

5 thin crackers (such as almond flour crackers, or flax crackers)

Directions

1. Combine salmon with pesto, yogurt, and shallot.

2. Serve over avocado and baby spinach with crackers on the side.

Pizza Omelette

Ingredients:

2 eggs

Sliced peppers

Sliced mushrooms

Onion

Flaxseed milk

Onion and garlic powder and pepper, to taste

1/2 Avocado

Lemon Juice

1 tbsp. olive oil

Directions

1. Sautee onions, peppers and mushrooms in olive oil.

2. Wisk eggs with flax seed milk, season with onion and garlic powder and pepper, then add to veggie mixture.

3. Gently push cooked portions towards the center. When the surface no longer has uncooked eggs, fold it in half.

4. Serve with mashed avocado drizzled with lemon juice.

Brick-Oven Pizza (Brooklyn Style)

Ingredients

- 1 teaspoon active dry yeast

- ¼ cup warm water

- 1 cup cold water

- 1 teaspoon salt

- 3 cups bread flour

- 6 ounces low moisture mozzarella cheese, thinly sliced

- ½ cup no salt added canned crushed tomatoes

- ¼ teaspoon freshly ground black pepper

- ½ teaspoon dried oregano

- 3 tablespoons extra-virgin olive oil

- 6 leaves fresh basil, torn

Directions

- Step 1

Sprinkle yeast over warm water in a large bowl. Let stand for 5 minutes to proof. Stir in salt and cold water, then stir in the flour about 1 cup at a time. When the dough is together enough to remove from the bowl, knead on a floured surface until smooth, about 10 minutes. Divide into two pieces, and form each one into a tight ball. Coat the dough balls with olive oil, and refrigerate in a sealed container for at least 16 hours. Be sure to use a big enough container to allow the dough to rise. Remove the dough from the refrigerator one hour prior to using.

- Step 2

Preheat the oven, with a pizza stone on the lowest rack, to 550 degrees F. Lightly dust a pizza peel with flour.

- Step 3

Using one ball of dough at a time, lightly dust the dough with flour, and stretch gradually until it is about 14 inches in diameter, or about as big around as the pizza stone. Place on the floured peel. Place thin slices of mozzarella over the crust, then grind a liberal amount of black pepper over it. Sprinkle with dried oregano. Randomly arrange crushed tomatoes, leaving some empty areas. Drizzle olive oil over the top.

• Step 4

With a quick back and forth jerk, make sure the dough will release from the peel easily. Place the tip of the peel at the back of the preheated pizza stone, and remove peel so that the pizza is left on the stone.

• Step 5

Bake for 4 to 6 minutes in the preheated oven, or until the crust begins to brown. Remove from the oven by sliding the peel beneath the pizza. Sprinkle a few basil leaves randomly over the pizza. Cut into wedges and serve.

Turkey Bolognese Sauce

Ingredients

- 2 pounds ground turkey

- 2 onions, minced

- 4 cloves garlic, minced

- ¾ cup grated carrots

- 1 ½ teaspoons dried basil

- 2 tablespoons minced jalapeno peppers

- 1 cup milk

- 1 ½ cups white wine

- 2 (28 ounce) cans whole peeled tomatoes

- 1 tablespoon tomato paste

- 1 pound spaghetti

- ½ cup grated Parmesan cheese

Directions

- Step 1

In large saucepan over medium heat, cook turkey, onion, garlic, carrot, basil and jalapeno until turkey is brown. Pour in milk, reduce heat to low, and simmer until reduced by one-third. Stir in wine and reduce again. Pour in tomatoes and tomato paste and simmer 3 hours more.

- Step 2

Bring a large pot of lightly salted water to a boil. Add pasta and cook for 8 to 10 minutes or until al dente; drain. Toss with tomato sauce and top with Parmesan.

Grilled Tuna Teriyaki

Ingredients

- 2 tablespoons light soy sauce

- 1 tablespoon Chinese rice wine

- 1 tablespoon minced fresh ginger root

- 1 large clove garlic, minced

- 4 (6 ounce) tuna steaks (about 3/4 inch thick)

- 1 tablespoon vegetable oil

Directions

- Step 1

Stir soy sauce, rice wine, ginger, and garlic together in a shallow dish. Place tuna in the marinade, and turn to coat. Cover dish and refrigerate for at least 30 minutes.

- Step 2

Preheat grill for medium-high heat.

- Step 3

Remove tuna from marinade and discard remaining liquid. Brush both sides of steaks with oil.

- Step 4

Cook tuna on the preheated grill until cooked through, 3 to 6 minutes per side.

Elegant Pork Loin Roast

Ingredients

- 1 (4 pound) boneless pork loin roast

- ¼ cup Dijon mustard

- 2 tablespoons packed brown sugar

- 1 ½ cups apple juice, divided

- 1 cup pitted prunes

- 1 cup dried apricots

- ¾ cup red wine

- ¼ cup packed brown sugar

- ⅛ teaspoon ground cloves

- 2 teaspoons cornstarch

- Step 1

Preheat the oven to 325 degrees F (165 degrees C).

- Step 2

Place the roast in a shallow roasting pan. Mix together the mustard and 2 tablespoons of brown sugar; spread over the roast.

- Step 3

Roast for 3 hours in the preheated oven, basting with 1/4 cup of apple juice every 30 minutes. Roast is done when the internal temperature reads 145 degrees F (63 degrees C).

- Step 4

During the last hour the roast is cooking, combine the prunes, apricots, red wine, 1/4 cup brown sugar, 3/4 cup of the juices from the roasting pan, and cloves in a saucepan over medium heat. Bring to a boil, then cover and simmer for 15 minutes. Spoon the fruit around the roast in the roasting pan during the last 30 minutes of cooking.

- Step 5

When the roast is done, place it onto a serving platter and spoon the fruit around it. Remove 1/4 cup of the drippings from the roasting pan, and mix with the cornstarch. Stir into the pan of drippings, and cook over medium-high heat, stirring gently until thickened and no longer cloudy, about 5 minutes. Transfer to a gravy boat or serving bowl.

- Step 6

Slice the roast, and pass the sauce for guests to serve themselves.

Szechwan Shrimp

Ingredients

- 4 tablespoons water

- 2 tablespoons ketchup

- 1 tablespoon soy sauce

- 2 teaspoons cornstarch

- 1 teaspoon honey

- ½ teaspoon crushed red pepper

- ¼ teaspoon ground ginger

- 1 tablespoon vegetable oil

- ¼ cup sliced green onions

- 4 cloves garlic, minced

- 12 ounces cooked shrimp, tails removed

Directions

- Step 1

In a bowl, stir together water, ketchup, soy sauce, cornstarch, honey, crushed red pepper, and ground ginger. Set aside.

Step 2

Heat oil in a large skillet over medium-high heat. Stir in green onions and garlic; cook 30 seconds. Stir in shrimp, and toss to coat with oil. Stir in sauce. Cook and stir until sauce is bubbly and thickened.

Ginger Glazed Mahi Mahi

Ingredients

- 3 tablespoons honey

- 3 tablespoons soy sauce

- 3 tablespoons balsamic vinegar

- 1 teaspoon grated fresh ginger root

- 1 clove garlic, crushed or to taste

- 2 teaspoons olive oil

- 4 (6 ounce) mahi mahi fillets

- salt and pepper to taste

- 1 tablespoon vegetable oil

Directions

• Step 1

In a shallow glass dish, stir together the honey, soy sauce, balsamic vinegar, ginger, garlic and olive oil. Season fish fillets with salt and pepper, and place them into the dish. If the fillets have skin on them, place them skin side down. Cover, and refrigerate for 20 minutes to marinate.

• Step 2

Heat vegetable oil in a large skillet over medium-high heat. Remove fish from the dish, and reserve marinade. Fry fish for 4 to 6 minutes on each side, turning only once, until fish flakes easily with a fork. Remove fillets to a serving platter and keep warm.

- Step 3

Pour reserved marinade into the skillet, and heat over medium heat until the mixture reduces to a glaze consistently. Spoon glaze over fish, and serve immediately.

Chicken with Garlic, Basil, and Parsley

Ingredients

- 1 tablespoon dried parsley, divided

- 1 tablespoon dried basil, divided

- 4 skinless, boneless chicken breast halves

- 4 cloves garlic, thinly sliced

- ½ teaspoon salt

- ½ teaspoon crushed red pepper flakes

- 2 tomatoes, sliced

Directions

- Step 1

Preheat oven to 350 degrees F (175 degrees C). Coat a 9x13 inch baking dish with cooking spray.

- Step 2

Sprinkle 1 teaspoon parsley and 1 teaspoon basil evenly over the bottom of the baking dish. Arrange chicken breast halves in the dish, and sprinkle evenly with garlic slices. In a small bowl, mix the remaining 2 teaspoons parsley, remaining 2 teaspoons basil, salt, and red pepper; sprinkle over the chicken. Top with tomato slices.

- Step 3

Bake covered in the preheated oven 25 minutes. Remove cover, and continue baking 15 minutes, or until chicken juices run clear.

Chinese Pork Chops

Ingredients

- ½ cup soy sauce

- ¼ cup brown sugar

- 2 tablespoons lemon juice

- 1 tablespoon vegetable oil

- ½ teaspoon ground ginger

- ⅛ teaspoon garlic powder

- 6 boneless pork chops

Directions

- Step 1

In a bowl, mix the soy sauce, brown sugar, lemon juice, vegetable oil, ginger, and garlic powder. Set aside some of the mixture in a separate bowl for marinating during cooking. Pierce the pork chops on both sides with a fork, place in a large resealable plastic bag, and cover with the remaining marinade mixture. Refrigerate 6 to 8 hours.

- Step 2

Preheat the grill for high heat.

- Step 3

Lightly oil the grill grate. Discard marinade, and grill pork chops 6 to 8 minutes per side, or to desired doneness, marinating often with the reserved portion of the marinade.

Honey-Dijon Chicken With A Kick

Ingredients

- 4 skinless, boneless chicken breast halves

- 1 tablespoon red pepper flakes

- ½ cup honey

- ¼ cup Dijon mustard

Directions

- Step 1

Preheat oven to 350 degrees F (175 degrees C).

- Step 2

Place chicken breasts in a baking dish; sprinkle with red pepper flakes. Mix honey and mustard in a small bowl and pour mixture over chicken. Cover baking dish with aluminum foil.

- Step 3

Bake in the preheated oven until the juices run clear and chicken is no longer pink inside, about 40 minutes. An instant-read meat thermometer inserted into the thickest part of a breast should read at least 160 degrees F (70 degrees C).

Portobello Mushroom Caps and Veggies

Ingredients

- 1 tablespoon olive oil

- 1 tablespoon garlic, peeled and minced

- 1 onion, cut into strips

- 1 green bell pepper, cut into strips

- ¼ teaspoon salt

- 4 large portobello mushroom caps

Directions

- Step 1

Heat olive oil in a medium skillet over medium heat. Stir in the garlic, onion, and green bell pepper. Season with salt. Cook about 5 minutes, until vegetables are tender.

- Step 2

Reduce skillet heat to low. Place mushroom caps in the skillet, cover, and cook about 5 minutes per side, until tender.

Grilled Pork Tenderloin

Ingredients

- 2 (1 pound) pork tenderloins

- 1 teaspoon garlic powder

- 1 teaspoon salt

- 1 teaspoon ground black pepper

- 1 cup barbeque sauce

Directions

- Step 1

Prepare grill for indirect heat.

- Step 2

Season meat with garlic powder, salt, and pepper.

- Step 3

Lightly oil grate. Place tenderloin on grate, and position drip pan under meat. Cook over indirect heat for 30 minutes.

- Step 4

Brush tenderloin with barbeque sauce. Continue cooking for 15 minutes, or until an instant-read thermometer inserted into the center reads 145 degrees F (63 degrees C). Allow pork to rest for 10 minutes. Slice pork, and serve with additional barbeque sauce for dipping.

Spicy Basil Chicken

- 2 tablespoons chili oil

- 2 cloves garlic

- 3 hot chile peppers

- 1 pound skinless, boneless chicken breast halves - cut into bite-size pieces

- 1 ½ teaspoons white sugar

- 1 teaspoon garlic salt

- 1 teaspoon black pepper

- 5 tablespoons oyster sauce

- 1 cup fresh mushrooms

- 1 cup chopped onions

- 1 bunch fresh basil leaves

Directions

- Step 1

Heat the oil in a skillet over medium-high heat, and cook the garlic and chile peppers until golden brown. Mix in chicken and sugar, and season with garlic salt and pepper. Cook until chicken is no longer pink, but not done.

- Step 2

Stir oyster sauce into the skillet. Mix in mushrooms and onions, and continue cooking until onions are tender and chicken juices run clear. Remove from heat, and mix in basil. Let sit 2 minutes before serving.

Homemade Black Bean Veggie Burgers

Ingredients

- 1 (16 ounce) can black beans, drained and rinsed

- ½ green bell pepper, cut into 2 inch pieces

- ½ onion, cut into wedges

- 3 cloves garlic, peeled

- 1 egg

- 1 tablespoon chili powder

- 1 tablespoon cumin

- 1 teaspoon Thai chili sauce or hot sauce

- ½ cup bread crumbs

Directions

- Step 1

If grilling, preheat an outdoor grill for high heat, and lightly oil a sheet of aluminum foil. If baking, preheat oven to 375 degrees F (190 degrees C), and lightly oil a baking sheet.

- Step 2

In a medium bowl, mash black beans with a fork until thick and pasty.

- Step 3

In a food processor, finely chop bell pepper, onion, and garlic. Then stir into mashed beans.

- Step 4

In a small bowl, stir together egg, chili powder, cumin, and chili sauce.

- Step 5

Stir the egg mixture into the mashed beans. Mix in bread crumbs until the mixture is sticky and holds together. Divide mixture into four patties.

- Step 6

If grilling, place patties on foil, and grill about 8 minutes on each side. If baking, place patties on baking sheet, and bake about 10 minutes on each side.

Hawaiian Chicken Kabobs

- 3 tablespoons soy sauce

- 3 tablespoons brown sugar

- 2 tablespoons sherry

- 1 tablespoon sesame oil

- ¼ teaspoon ground ginger

- ¼ teaspoon garlic powder

- 8 skinless, boneless chicken breast halves - cut into 2 inch pieces

- 1 (20 ounce) can pineapple chunks, drained

- skewers

Directions

- Step 1

In a shallow glass dish, mix the soy sauce, brown sugar, sherry, sesame oil, ginger, and garlic powder. Stir the chicken pieces and pineapple into the marinade until well coated. Cover, and marinate in the refrigerator at least 2 hours.

- Step 2

Preheat grill to medium-high heat.

- Step 3

Lightly oil the grill grate. Thread chicken and pineapple alternately onto skewers. Grill 15 to 20 minutes, turning occasionally, or until chicken juices run clear.

Mustard Crusted Tilapia

Ingredients

- 2 (6 ounce) fresh tilapia fillets

- 1 teaspoon spicy brown mustard

- 1 teaspoon Worcestershire sauce

- ½ teaspoon lemon juice

- ¼ teaspoon garlic powder

- ¼ teaspoon dried oregano

- ½ teaspoon grated Parmesan cheese

- 1 teaspoon fine Italian bread crumbs

Directions

- Step 1

Preheat oven to 375 degrees F (190 degrees C). Spray a glass baking dish with cooking spray.

- Step 2

Place tilapia fillets into prepared baking dish, and bake in preheated oven for 10 minutes. Meanwhile, stir together the mustard, Worcestershire sauce, lemon juice, garlic powder, oregano, and Parmesan cheese.

- Step 3

When fish has cooked for 10 minutes, spread with herb paste, and sprinkle with bread crumbs. Continue baking for another

5 minutes until the topping is bubbly and golden.

Pesto Pasta

Ingredients

- ½ cup chopped onion

- 2 ½ tablespoons pesto

- 2 tablespoons olive oil

- 2 tablespoons grated Parmesan cheese

- 1 (16 ounce) package pasta

- salt to taste

- ground black pepper to taste

Directions

- Step 1

Cook pasta in a large pot of boiling water until done. Drain.

- Step 2

Meanwhile, heat the oil in a frying pan over medium low heat. Add pesto, onion, and salt and pepper. Cook about five minutes, or until onions are soft.

- Step 3

In a large bowl, mix pesto mixture into pasta. Stir in grated cheese. Serve.

California Melt

Ingredients

- 4 slices whole-grain bread, lightly toasted

- 1 avocado, sliced

- 1 cup sliced mushrooms

- ⅓ cup sliced toasted almonds

- 1 tomato, sliced

- 4 slices Swiss cheese

Directions

- Step 1

Preheat the oven broiler.

- Step 2

Lay the toasted bread out on a baking sheet. Top each slice of bread with 1/4 of the avocado, mushrooms, almonds, and tomato slices. Top each with a slice of Swiss cheese.

- Step 3

Broil the open-face sandwiches until the cheese melts and begins to bubble, about 2 minutes. Serve the sandwiches warm.

Fluffy French Toast

Ingredients

- ¼ cup all-purpose flour
- 1 cup milk
- 1 pinch salt
- 3 eggs
- ½ teaspoon ground cinnamon
- 1 teaspoon vanilla extract
- 1 tablespoon white sugar
- 12 thick slices bread

Directions

- Step 1

Measure flour into a large mixing bowl. Slowly whisk in the milk. Whisk in the salt, eggs, cinnamon, vanilla extract and sugar until smooth.

- Step 2

Heat a lightly oiled griddle or frying pan over medium heat.

- Step 3

Soak bread slices in mixture until saturated. Cook bread on each side until golden brown. Serve hot.

Amazing Pork Tenderloin in the Slow Cooker

Ingredients

- 1 (2 pound) pork tenderloin

- 1 (1 ounce) envelope dry onion soup mix

- 1 cup water

- ¾ cup red wine

- 3 tablespoons minced garlic

- 3 tablespoons soy sauce

- freshly ground black pepper to taste

Directions

- Step 1

Place pork tenderloin in a slow cooker with the contents of the soup packet. Pour water, wine, and soy sauce over the top, turning the pork to coat. Carefully spread garlic over the pork, leaving as much on top of the roast during cooking as possible. Sprinkle with pepper, cover, and cook on low setting for 4 hours. Serve with cooking liquid on the side as au jus.

Black Beans and Rice

Ingredients

- 1 teaspoon olive oil

- 1 onion, chopped

- 2 cloves garlic, minced

- ¾ cup uncooked white rice

- 1 ½ cups low sodium, low fat vegetable broth

- 1 teaspoon ground cumin

- ¼ teaspoon cayenne pepper

- 3 ½ cups canned black beans, drained

Directions

- Step 1

In a stockpot over medium-high heat, heat the oil. Add the onion and garlic and saute for 4 minutes. Add the rice and saute for 2 minutes.

- Step 2

Add the vegetable broth, bring to a boil, cover and lower the heat and cook for 20 minutes. Add the spices and black beans.

Fish in Foil

Ingredients

- 2 rainbow trout fillets

- 1 tablespoon olive oil

- 2 teaspoons garlic salt

- 1 teaspoon ground black pepper

- 1 fresh jalapeno pepper, sliced

- 1 lemon, sliced

Directions

- Step 1

Preheat oven to 400 degrees F (200 degrees C). Rinse fish, and pat dry.

- Step 2

Rub fillets with olive oil, and season with garlic salt and black pepper. Place each fillet on a large sheet of aluminum foil. Top with jalapeno slices, and squeeze the juice from the ends of the lemons over the fish. Arrange lemon slices on top of fillets. Carefully seal all edges of the foil to form enclosed packets. Place packets on baking sheet.

- Step 3

Bake in preheated oven for 15 to 20 minutes, depending on the size of fish. Fish is done when it flakes easily with a fork.

Blackened Chicken

Ingredients

- ½ teaspoon paprika

- ⅛ teaspoon salt

- ¼ teaspoon cayenne pepper

- ¼ teaspoon ground cumin

- ¼ teaspoon dried thyme

- ⅛ teaspoon ground white pepper

- ⅛ teaspoon onion powder

- 2 skinless, boneless chicken breast halves

Directions

- Step 1

Preheat oven to 350 degrees F (175 degrees C). Lightly grease a baking sheet. Heat a cast iron skillet over high heat for 5 minutes until it is smoking hot.

- Step 2

Mix together the paprika, salt, cayenne, cumin, thyme, white pepper, and onion powder. Oil the chicken breasts with cooking spray on both sides, then coat the chicken breasts evenly with the spice mixture.

- Step 3

Place the chicken in the hot pan, and cook for 1 minute. Turn, and cook 1 minute on other side. Place the breasts on the prepared baking sheet.

- Step 4

Bake in the preheated oven until no longer pink in the center and the juices run clear, about 5 minutes.

Pesto Pasta with Chicken

Ingredients

- 1 (16 ounce) package bow tie pasta

- 1 teaspoon olive oil

- 2 cloves garlic, minced

- 2 boneless skinless chicken breasts, cut into bite-size pieces

- crushed red pepper flakes to taste

- ⅓ cup oil-packed sun-dried tomatoes, drained and cut into strips

- ½ cup pesto sauce

Directions

- Step 1

Bring a large pot of lightly salted water to a boil. Add pasta and cook for 8 to 10 minutes or until al dente; drain.

- Step 2

Heat oil in a large skillet over medium heat. Saute garlic until tender, then stir in chicken. Season with red pepper flakes. Cook until chicken is golden, and cooked through.

- Step 3

In a large bowl, combine pasta, chicken, sun-dried tomatoes and pesto. Toss to coat evenly.

Easy Baked Tilapia

Ingredients

- 4 (4 ounce) fillets tilapia

- 2 teaspoons butter

- ¼ teaspoon Old Bay Seasoning TM, or to taste

- ½ teaspoon garlic salt, or to taste

- 1 lemon, sliced

- 1 (16 ounce) package frozen cauliflower with broccoli and red pepper

Directions

- Step 1

Preheat the oven to 375 degrees F (190 degrees F). Grease a 9x13 inch baking dish.

- Step 2

Place the tilapia fillets in the bottom of the baking dish and dot with butter. Season with Old Bay seasoning and garlic salt. Top each one with a slice or two of lemon. Arrange the frozen mixed vegetables around the fish, and season lightly with salt and pepper.

- Step 3

Cover the dish and bake for 25 to 30 minutes in the preheated oven, until vegetables are tender and fish flakes easily with a fork.

Baked Honey Mustard Chicken

Ingredients

- 6 skinless, boneless chicken breast halves

- salt and pepper to taste

- ½ cup honey

- ½ cup prepared mustard

- 1 teaspoon dried basil

- 1 teaspoon paprika

- ½ teaspoon dried parsley

Directions

- Step 1

Preheat oven to 350 degrees F (175 degrees C).

- Step 2

Sprinkle chicken breasts with salt and pepper to taste, and place in a lightly greased 9x13 inch baking dish. In a small bowl, combine the honey, mustard, basil, paprika, and parsley. Mix well. Pour 1/2 of this mixture over the chicken, and brush to cover.

- Step 3

Bake in the preheated oven for 30 minutes. Turn chicken pieces over and brush with the remaining 1/2 of the honey mustard mixture. Bake for an additional 10 to 15 minutes, or until chicken is no longer pink and juices run clear. Let cool 10 minutes before serving.

RamJam Chicken

Ingredients

- ¼ cup soy sauce

- 3 tablespoons dry white wine

- 2 tablespoons lemon juice

- 2 tablespoons vegetable oil

- ¾ teaspoon dried Italian-style seasoning

- 1 teaspoon grated fresh ginger root

- 1 clove garlic, crushed

- ¼ teaspoon onion powder

- 1 pinch ground black pepper

- 8 skinless, boneless chicken breast halves - cut into strips

Directions

- Step 1

In a large, resealable plastic bag, combine the soy sauce, wine, lemon juice, oil, Italian-style seasoning, ginger, garlic, onion powder, and ground black pepper. Place chicken in the bag. Seal, and let marinate in the refrigerator for at least 3 hours, or overnight.

- Step 2

Preheat an outdoor grill for medium-high heat.

- Step 3

Thread the chicken onto skewers, and set aside. Pour marinade into a small saucepan, and bring to a boil over high heat.

- Step 4

Lightly oil the grill grate. Cook chicken on the prepared grill for approximately 8 minutes per side, basting with the sauce several times. Chicken is done when juices run clear.

Ginger Veggie Stir-Fry

Ingredients

- 1 tablespoon cornstarch

- 1 ½ cloves garlic, crushed

- 2 teaspoons chopped fresh ginger root, divided

- ¼ cup vegetable oil, divided

- 1 small head broccoli, cut into florets

- ½ cup snow peas

- ¾ cup julienned carrots

- ½ cup halved green beans

- 2 tablespoons soy sauce

- 2 ½ tablespoons water

- ¼ cup chopped onion

- ½ tablespoon salt

Directions

- Step 1

In a large bowl, blend cornstarch, garlic, 1 teaspoon ginger, and 2 tablespoons vegetable oil until cornstarch is dissolved.

Mix in broccoli, snow peas, carrots, and green beans, tossing to lightly coat.

- Step 2

Heat remaining 2 tablespoons oil in a large skillet or wok over medium heat. Cook vegetables in oil for 2 minutes, stirring constantly to prevent burning. Stir in soy sauce and water. Mix in onion, salt, and remaining 1 teaspoon ginger. Cook until vegetables are tender but still crisp.

Apple Cinnamon Oatmeal

Ingredients

- 1 cup water

- ¼ cup apple juice

- 1 apple, cored and chopped

- ⅔ cup rolled oats

- 1 teaspoon ground cinnamon

- 1 cup milk

Directions

- Step 1

Combine the water, apple juice, and apples in a saucepan. Bring to a boil over high heat, and stir in the rolled oats and cinnamon. Return to a boil, then reduce heat to low, and simmer until thick, about 3 minutes. Spoon into serving bowls, and pour milk over the servings.

Red Lentil Curry

Ingredients

- 2 cups red lentils

- 1 large onion, diced

- 1 tablespoon vegetable oil

- 2 tablespoons curry paste

- 1 tablespoon curry powder

- 1 teaspoon ground turmeric

- 1 teaspoon ground cumin

- 1 teaspoon chili powder

- 1 teaspoon salt

- 1 teaspoon white sugar

- 1 teaspoon minced garlic

- 1 teaspoon minced fresh ginger

- 1 (14.25 ounce) can tomato puree

Directions

- Step 1

Wash the lentils in cold water until the water runs clear. Put lentils in a pot with enough water to cover; bring to a boil, place a cover on the pot, reduce heat to medium-low, and simmer, adding water during cooking as needed to keep covered, until tender, 15 to 20 minutes. Drain.

- Step 2

Heat vegetable oil in a large skillet over medium heat; cook and stir onions in hot oil until caramelized, about 20 minutes.

- Step 3

Mix curry paste, curry powder, turmeric, cumin, chili powder, salt, sugar, garlic, and ginger together in a large bowl; stir into the onions. Increase heat to high and cook, stirring constantly, until fragrant, 1 to 2 minutes.

- Step 4

Stir in the tomato puree, remove from heat and stir into the lentils.

Turkey Veggie Meatloaf Cups

Ingredients

- 2 cups coarsely chopped zucchini

- 1 ½ cups coarsely chopped onions

- 1 red bell pepper, coarsely chopped

- 1 pound extra lean ground turkey

- ½ cup uncooked couscous

- 1 egg

- 2 tablespoons Worcestershire sauce

- 1 tablespoon Dijon mustard

- ½ cup barbecue sauce, or as needed

Directions

Instructions Checklist

- Step 1

Preheat oven to 400 degrees F (200 degrees C). Spray 20 muffin cups with cooking spray.

- Step 2

Place zucchini, onions, and red bell pepper into a food processor, and pulse several times until finely chopped but not liquefied. Place the vegetables into a bowl, and mix in ground turkey, couscous, egg, Worcestershire sauce, and Dijon mustard until thoroughly combined. Fill each prepared muffin cup about 3/4 full. Top each cup with about 1 teaspoon of barbecue sauce.

- Step 3

Bake in the preheated oven until juices run clear, about 25 minutes. Internal temperature of a muffin measured by an instant-read meat thermometer should be at least 160 degrees F (70 degrees C). Let stand 5 minutes before serving.

Lemon Garlic Tilapia

Ingredients

- 4 each tilapia fillets

- 3 tablespoons fresh lemon juice

- 1 tablespoon butter, melted

- 1 clove garlic, finely chopped

- 1 teaspoon dried parsley flakes

- 1 dash pepper to taste

Directions

- Step 1

Preheat oven to 375 degrees F (190 degrees C). Spray a baking dish with non-stick cooking spray.

- Step 2

Rinse tilapia fillets under cool water, and pat dry with paper towels.

- Step 3

Place fillets in baking dish. Pour lemon juice over fillets, then drizzle butter on top. Sprinkle with garlic, parsley, and pepper.

- Step 4

Bake in preheated oven until the fish is white and flakes when pulled apart with a fork, about 30 minutes.

Chicken Kabobs

Ingredients

- 4 skinless, boneless chicken breast halves - cubed

- 1 large green bell pepper, cut into 2 inch pieces

- 1 onion, cut into wedges

- 1 large red bell pepper, cut into 2 inch pieces

- 1 cup barbeque sauce

- skewers

Directions

- Step 1

Preheat grill for high heat.

- Step 2

Thread the chicken, green bell pepper, onion, and red bell pepper pieces onto skewers alternately.

- Step 3

Lightly oil the grill grate. Place kabobs on the prepared grill, and brush with barbeque sauce. Cook, turning and brushing with barbeque sauce frequently, for 15 minutes, or until chicken juices run clear.

Ingredients

- 4 skinless, boneless chicken breast halves - cubed

- 1 large green bell pepper, cut into 2 inch pieces

- 1 onion, cut into wedges

- 1 large red bell pepper, cut into 2 inch pieces

- 1 cup barbeque sauce

- skewers

Directions

- Step 1

Preheat grill for high heat.

- Step 2

Thread the chicken, green bell pepper, onion, and red bell pepper pieces onto skewers alternately.

- Step 3

Lightly oil the grill grate. Place kabobs on the prepared grill, and brush with barbeque sauce. Cook, turning and brushing with barbeque sauce frequently, for 15 minutes, or until chicken juices run clear.

Spicy Chicken Breasts

Ingredients

- 2 ½ tablespoons paprika

- 2 tablespoons garlic powder

- 1 tablespoon salt

- 1 tablespoon onion powder

- 1 tablespoon dried thyme

- 1 tablespoon ground cayenne pepper

- 1 tablespoon ground black pepper

- 4 skinless, boneless chicken breast halves

Directions

- Step 1

In a medium bowl, mix together the paprika, garlic powder, salt, onion powder, thyme, cayenne pepper, and ground black pepper. Set aside about 3 tablespoons of this seasoning mixture for the chicken; store the remainder in an airtight container for later use (for seasoning fish, meats, or vegetables).

- Step 2

Preheat grill for medium-high heat. Rub some of the reserved 3 tablespoons of seasoning onto both sides of the chicken breasts.

- Step 3

Lightly oil the grill grate. Place chicken on the grill, and cook for 6 to 8 minutes on each side, until juices run clear.

Spaghetti Squash I

Ingredients

- 1 spaghetti squash, halved lengthwise and seeded

- 2 tablespoons vegetable oil

- 1 onion, chopped

- 1 clove garlic, minced

- 1 ½ cups chopped tomatoes

- ¾ cup crumbled feta cheese

- 3 tablespoons sliced black olives

- 2 tablespoons chopped fresh basil

Directions

- Step 1

Preheat oven to 350 degrees F (175 degrees C). Lightly grease a baking sheet.

- Step 2

Place spaghetti squash with cut sides down on the prepared baking sheet, and bake 30 minutes in the preheated oven, or until a sharp knife can be inserted with only a little resistance. Remove squash from oven and set aside to cool enough to be easily handled.

- Step 3

Meanwhile, heat oil in a skillet over medium heat. Cook and stir onion in oil until tender. Add garlic; cook and stir until fragrant, 2 to 3 minutes. Stir in tomatoes and cook until tomatoes are warmed through.

- Step 4

Use a large spoon to scoop the stringy pulp from the squash and place in a medium bowl. Toss with the vegetables, feta cheese, olives, and basil. Serve warm.

Easy Slow Cooker Meatballs

Ingredients

- 1 ½ pounds ground beef

- 1 ¼ cups Italian seasoned bread crumbs

- ¼ cup chopped fresh parsley

- 2 cloves garlic, minced

- 1 medium yellow onion, chopped

- 1 egg, beaten

- 1 (28 ounce) jar spaghetti sauce

- 1 (16 ounce) can crushed tomatoes

- 1 (14.25 ounce) can tomato puree

Directions

- Step 1

In a bowl, mix the ground beef, bread crumbs, parsley, garlic, onion, and egg. Shape the mixture into 16 meatballs.

- Step 2

In a slow cooker, mix the spaghetti sauce, crushed tomatoes, and tomato puree. Place the meatballs into the sauce mixture. Cook on Low for 6 to 8 hours.

Ginger Glazed Mahi Mahi

Ingredients

- 3 tablespoons honey

- 3 tablespoons soy sauce

- 3 tablespoons balsamic vinegar

- 1 teaspoon grated fresh ginger root

- 1 clove garlic, crushed or to taste

- 2 teaspoons olive oil

- 4 (6 ounce) mahi mahi fillets

- salt and pepper to taste

- 1 tablespoon vegetable oil

Directions

- Step 1

In a shallow glass dish, stir together the honey, soy sauce, balsamic vinegar, ginger, garlic and olive oil. Season fish fillets with salt and pepper, and place them into the dish. If the fillets have skin on them, place them skin side down. Cover, and refrigerate for 20 minutes to marinate.

- Step 2

Heat vegetable oil in a large skillet over medium-high heat. Remove fish from the dish, and reserve marinade. Fry fish for 4 to 6 minutes on each side, turning only once, until fish flakes easily with a fork. Remove fillets to a serving platter and keep warm.

- Step 3

Pour reserved marinade into the skillet, and heat over medium heat until the mixture reduces to a glaze consistently. Spoon glaze over fish, and serve immediately.

Garlic Shrimp Linguine

Ingredients

- 1 pound uncooked linguine

- 1 tablespoon butter

- 3 tablespoons white wine

- 2 teaspoons grated Parmesan cheese

- 3 cloves garlic, minced

- 1 teaspoon chopped fresh parsley

- 1 pinch salt and pepper to taste

- 1 pound medium shrimp, peeled and deveined

Directions

- Step 1

Bring a large pot of lightly salted water to a boil. Add pasta and cook for 8 to 10 minutes or until al dente; drain.

- Step 2

In a medium saucepan, melt butter over medium low heat; add wine, cheese, garlic, parsley and salt and pepper to taste. Simmer over low heat for 3 to 5 minutes, stirring frequently.

- Step 3

Increase heat to medium high and add shrimp to saucepan; cook for about 3 to 4 minutes or until shrimp begins to turn pink. Do not overcook.

- Step 4

Divide pasta into portions and spoon sauce on top; garnish with Parmesan cheese and fresh parsley, if desired.

Utokia's Ginger Shrimp and Broccoli with Garlic

Ingredients

- Reynolds® Parchment Paper

- 4 cups broccoli florets

- 1 pound raw shrimp, peeled and deveined

- 2 cloves garlic, crushed

- 1 tablespoon sesame oil

- ½ tablespoon grated fresh ginger

- ½ tablespoon soy sauce

Directions

- Step 1

Preheat oven to 400 degrees F. Tear off four 15-inch sheets of Reynolds Parchment Paper. Fold each sheet in half and crease it in the center. Cut each into a heart shape; unfold.

- Step 2

Divide broccoli and shrimp evenly on one-half of each sheet near crease.

- Step 3

Mix garlic, sesame oil, ginger and soy sauce. Spoon 1/4 the mixture evenly over broccoli and shrimp on each sheet.

- Step 4

Fold over other half of each sheet to enclose ingredients. Starting at top, make small overlapping folds down entire length of parchment to secure edges together. Twist last fold several times to make a tight seal. Place parchment packets on a large baking sheet with 1-inch sides.

- Step 5

Bake 13 to 15 minutes or until shrimp is done.

- Step 6

Place parchment packets on dinner plates. Carefully cut an X in the top of each packet;

open carefully, allowing steam to escape. Serve immediately.

Mediterranean Chicken

Ingredients

- 2 teaspoons olive oil

- 2 tablespoons white wine

- 6 skinless, boneless chicken breast halves

- 3 cloves garlic, minced

- ½ cup diced onion

- 3 cups tomatoes, chopped

- ½ cup white wine

- 2 teaspoons chopped fresh thyme

- 1 tablespoon chopped fresh basil

- ½ cup kalamata olives

- ¼ cup chopped fresh parsley

- salt and pepper to taste

Directions

- Step 1

Heat the oil and 2 tablespoons white wine in a large skillet over medium heat. Add chicken and saute about 4 to 6 minutes each side, until golden. Remove chicken from skillet and set aside.

- Step 2

Saute garlic in pan drippings for 30 seconds, then add onion and saute for 3 minutes. Add tomatoes and bring to a boil. Lower heat, add 1/2 cup white wine and simmer for 10 minutes. Add thyme and basil and simmer for 5 more minutes.

- Step 3

Return chicken to skillet and cover. Cook over low heat until the chicken is cooked through and no longer pink inside. Add olives and parsley to the skillet and cook for 1 minute. Season with salt and pepper to taste and serve.

Slow Cooker Cilantro Lime Chicken

Ingredients

- 1 (16 ounce) jar salsa

- 1 (1.25 ounce) package dry taco seasoning mix

- 1 lime, juiced

- 3 tablespoons chopped fresh cilantro

- 3 pounds skinless, boneless chicken breast halves

Directions

- Step 1

Place the salsa, taco seasoning, lime juice, and cilantro into a slow cooker, and stir to combine. Add the chicken breasts, and stir to coat with the salsa mixture. Cover the cooker, set to High, and cook until the chicken is very tender, about 4 hours. If desired, set cooker to Low and cook 6 to 8 hours. Shred chicken with 2 forks to serve.

Easy Cola Chicken

Ingredients

- 4 skinless, boneless chicken breast halves

- salt and pepper to taste

- 2 tablespoons Worcestershire sauce

- 1 cup ketchup

- 1 cup cola-flavored carbonated beverage

Directions

- Step 1

Preheat the oven to 350 degrees F (175 degrees C).

- Step 2

Place the chicken pieces into a 9x13 inch baking dish. Season with salt and pepper. In a medium bowl, mix together the Worcestershire sauce, ketchup and cola. Pour over the chicken. Cover with a lid or aluminum foil.

- Step 3

Bake for 50 minutes in the preheated oven, until the chicken is no longer pink.

Porridge

Ingredients

- 1 cup rolled oats

- 2 ½ cups water

- 1 teaspoon salt

- 1 tablespoon white sugar

- 2 bananas, sliced

- 1 pinch ground cinnamon

- ½ cup cold milk (Optional)

Directions

- Step 1

In a saucepan, combine the oats, water, salt, sugar, bananas and cinnamon. Bring to a boil, then reduce heat to low, and simmer until the liquid has been absorbed, stirring frequently. Pour into bowls, and top each with a splash of cold milk.

Jamaican Jerk Chicken

Ingredients

- 6 skinless, boneless chicken breast halves
- cut into chunks

- 4 limes, juiced

- 1 cup water

- 2 teaspoons ground allspice

- ½ teaspoon ground nutmeg

- 1 teaspoon salt

- 1 teaspoon brown sugar

- 2 teaspoons dried thyme

- 1 teaspoon ground ginger

- 1 ½ teaspoons ground black pepper

- 2 tablespoons vegetable oil

- 2 onions, chopped

- 1 ½ cups chopped green onions

- 6 cloves garlic, chopped

- 2 habanero peppers, chopped

Directions

- Step 1

Place chicken in a medium bowl. Cover with lime juice and water. Set aside.

- Step 2

In a blender or food processor, place allspice, nutmeg, salt, brown sugar, thyme, ginger, black pepper and vegetable oil. Blend well, then mix in onions, green onions, garlic and habanero peppers until almost smooth.

- Step 3

Pour most of the blended marinade mixture into bowl with chicken, reserving a small amount to use as a basting sauce while cooking. Cover, and marinate in the refrigerator for at least 2 hours.

- Step 4

Preheat an outdoor grill for medium heat.

- Step 5

Brush grill grate with oil. Cook chicken slowly on the preheated grill. Turn frequently, basting often with remaining marinade mixture. Cook to desired doneness.

Chicken in a Pot

Ingredients

- ¾ cup chicken broth

- 1 ½ tablespoons tomato paste

- ¼ teaspoon ground black pepper

- ½ teaspoon dried oregano

- ⅛ teaspoon salt

- 1 clove garlic, minced

- 4 boneless, skinless chicken breast halves

- 3 tablespoons dry bread crumbs

- 2 teaspoons olive oil

- 2 cups fresh sliced mushrooms

Directions

- Step 1

In a medium bowl, combine the broth, tomato paste, ground black pepper, oregano, salt and garlic. Mix well and set aside.

- Step 2

Dredge the chicken in the bread crumbs, coating well. Heat the oil in a large skillet over medium high heat. Saute the chicken in the oil for 2 minutes per side, or until lightly browned.

- Step 3

Add the reserved broth mixture and the mushrooms to the skillet and bring to a boil. Then cover, reduce heat to low and simmer for 20 minutes. Remove chicken and set aside, covering to keep it warm.

- Step 4

Bring broth mixture to a boil and cook for 4 minutes, or until reduced to desired thickness. Spoon sauce over the chicken and serve.

Leftover Chicken Croquettes

Ingredients

- 3 cups cooked, finely chopped chicken meat

- 1 ½ cups seasoned dry bread crumbs

- 2 eggs, lightly beaten

- 2 cups sauteed chopped onion

- 1 tablespoon chopped fresh parsley

- 1 teaspoon salt

- ½ teaspoon ground black pepper

Directions

- Step 1

In a large bowl combine the chicken, bread crumbs, 2 eggs and onion and mix well; if mixture is too dry to form patties, mix in another lightly beaten egg. Then add parsley, salt and pepper to taste, mix well and form into small patties.

- Step 2

Heat oil in a large skillet over medium heat and fry patties in oil until golden brown.

Steelhead Trout Bake with Dijon Mustard

Ingredients

- cooking spray

- 1 pound skinless steelhead trout fillets

- ¼ cup dry white wine

- 2 ½ tablespoons Dijon mustard

- 2 cloves garlic, pressed

- 1 tablespoon lemon juice

- 1 teaspoon dried dill weed

- 1 teaspoon lemon-pepper seasoning

Directions

- Step 1

Preheat oven to 400 degrees F (200 degrees C). Spray a 9x13-inch baking dish with cooking spray.

- Step 2

Arrange trout fillets in the baking dish. Mix white wine, Dijon mustard, garlic, lemon juice, dill, and lemon-pepper seasoning in a bowl; spread over the fillets, letting some run underneath the fish.

- Step 3

Bake in the preheated oven until the fish is opaque and flakes easily, 10 to 15 minutes.

Braised Balsamic Chicken

Ingredients

- 6 skinless, boneless chicken breast halves

- 1 teaspoon garlic salt

- ground black pepper to taste

- 2 tablespoons olive oil

- 1 onion, thinly sliced

- 1 (14.5 ounce) can diced tomatoes

- ½ cup balsamic vinegar

- 1 teaspoon dried basil

- 1 teaspoon dried oregano

- 1 teaspoon dried rosemary

- ½ teaspoon dried thyme

Directions

- Step 1

Season both sides of chicken breasts with garlic salt and pepper.

- Step 2

Heat olive oil in a skillet over medium heat; cook seasoned chicken breasts until chicken is browned, 3 to 4 minutes per side. Add onion; cook and stir until onion is browned, 3 to 4 minutes.

- Step 3

Pour diced tomatoes and balsamic vinegar over chicken; season with basil, oregano, rosemary and thyme. Simmer until chicken is no longer pink and the juices run clear, about 15 minutes. An instant-read thermometer inserted into the center should read at least 165 degrees F (74 degrees C).

Chicken Satay

Ingredients

- 2 tablespoons creamy peanut butter

- ½ cup soy sauce

- ½ cup lemon or lime juice

- 1 tablespoon brown sugar

- 2 tablespoons curry powder

- 2 cloves garlic, chopped

- 1 teaspoon hot pepper sauce

- 6 skinless, boneless chicken breast halves - cubed

Directions

- Step 1

In a mixing bowl, combine peanut butter, soy sauce, lime juice, brown sugar, curry powder, garlic and hot pepper sauce. Place the chicken breasts in the marinade and refrigerate. Let the chicken marinate at least 2 hours, overnight is best.

- Step 2

Preheat a grill to high heat.

- Step 3

Weave the chicken onto skewers, then grill for 5 minutes per side.

Maple-Garlic Marinated Pork Tenderloin

Ingredients

- 2 tablespoons Dijon mustard

- 1 teaspoon sesame oil

- 3 cloves garlic, minced

- fresh ground black pepper to taste

- 1 cup maple syrup

- 1 ½ pounds pork tenderloin

Directions

- Step 1

Combine mustard, sesame oil, garlic, pepper, and maple syrup. Place pork in a shallow dish and coat thoroughly with marinade. Cover, then chill in the refrigerator at least eight hours, or overnight.

- Step 2

Preheat grill for medium-low heat.

- Step 3

Remove pork from marinade, and set aside. Transfer remaining marinade to a small saucepan, and cook on the stove over medium-low heat for 5 minutes.

- Step 4

Brush grate with oil, and place meat on grate. Grill pork, basting with reserved marinade, for approximately 15 to 25 minutes, or until interior is no longer pink. Avoid using high temperatures as marinade will burn.

Fiery Fish Tacos with Crunchy Corn Salsa

Ingredients

- 2 cups cooked corn kernels

- ½ cup diced red onion

- 1 cup peeled, diced jicama

- ½ cup diced red bell pepper

- 1 cup fresh cilantro leaves, chopped

- 1 lime, juiced and zested

- 2 tablespoons cayenne pepper, or to taste

- 1 tablespoon ground black pepper

- 2 tablespoons salt, or to taste

- 6 (4 ounce) fillets tilapia

- 2 tablespoons olive oil

- 12 corn tortillas, warmed

- 2 tablespoons sour cream, or to taste

Directions

- Step 1

Preheat grill for high heat.

- Step 2

In a medium bowl, mix together corn, red onion, jicama, red bell pepper, and cilantro. Stir in lime juice and zest.

- Step 3

In a small bowl, combine cayenne pepper, ground black pepper, and salt.

- Step 4

Brush each fillet with olive oil, and sprinkle with spices to taste.

- Step 5

Arrange fillets on grill grate, and cook for 3 minutes per side. For each fiery fish taco, top two corn tortillas with fish, sour cream, and corn salsa.

Grilled Asian Ginger Pork Chops

Ingredients

- ½ cup orange juice

- 2 tablespoons soy sauce

- 2 tablespoons minced fresh ginger root

- 2 tablespoons grated orange zest

- 1 teaspoon minced garlic

- 1 teaspoon garlic chile paste

- ½ teaspoon salt

- 6 pork loin chops, 1/2 inch thick

Directions

- Step 1

In a shallow container, mix together orange juice, soy sauce, ginger, orange zest, garlic, chile paste, and salt. Add pork chops, and turn to coat evenly. Cover, and refrigerate for at least 2 hours, or overnight. Turn the pork chops in the marinade occasionally.

- Step 2

Preheat grill for high heat, and lightly oil grate.

- Step 3

Grill pork chops for 5 to 6 minutes per side, or to desired doneness.

Easy Garlic and Rosemary Chicken

Ingredients

- 2 skinless, boneless chicken breasts

- 2 cloves garlic, chopped

- 2 tablespoons dried rosemary

- 1 tablespoon lemon juice

- salt and pepper to taste

Directions

- Step 1

Preheat oven to 375 degrees F (190 degrees C).

- Step 2

Cover the chicken breasts with garlic, then sprinkle with rosemary, lemon juice, and salt and pepper to taste. Place in a 9x13 inch baking dish and bake in the preheated oven for 25 minutes or until done and juices run clear (baking time will depend on the thickness of your chicken breasts).

Slow Cooker Chicken Cacciatore

Ingredients

- 6 skinless, boneless chicken breast halves

- 1 (28 ounce) jar spaghetti sauce

- 2 green bell pepper, seeded and cubed

- 8 ounces fresh mushrooms, sliced

- 1 onion, finely diced

- 2 tablespoons minced garlic

Directions

- Step 1

Put the chicken in the slow cooker. Top with the spaghetti sauce, green bell peppers, mushrooms, onion, and garlic.

- Step 2

Cover, and cook on Low for 7 to 9 hours.

Pineapple Chicken Tenders

Ingredients

- 1 cup pineapple juice

- ½ cup packed brown sugar

- ⅓ cup light soy sauce

- 2 pounds chicken breast tenderloins or strips

- skewers

Directions

- Step 1

In a small saucepan over medium heat, mix pineapple juice, brown sugar, and soy sauce. Remove from heat just before the mixture comes to a boil.

- Step 2

Place chicken tenders in a medium bowl. Cover with the pineapple marinade, and refrigerate for at least 30 minutes.

- Step 3

Preheat grill for medium heat. Thread chicken lengthwise onto wooden skewers.

- Step 4

Lightly oil the grill grate. Grill chicken tenders 5 minutes per side, or until juices run clear. They cook quickly, so watch them closely.

Pineapple Pork Chops

Ingredients

- 1 tablespoon olive oil

- 4 boneless pork chops

- 1 (14.5 ounce) can chicken broth

- 2 tablespoons soy sauce

- 1 tablespoon vinegar

- 2 tablespoons brown sugar

- 2 tablespoons cornstarch

- ½ cup pineapple juice

Directions

- Step 1

Heat the olive oil in a skillet over medium heat, and brown the pork chops about 5 minutes on each side. Remove chops from the skillet, and set aside.

- Step 2

Mix the chicken broth, soy sauce and vinegar into the skillet, and bring to a boil. Return the pork chops to the skillet, reduce heat, and simmer 20 minutes. An instant-read thermometer inserted into the center should read 145 degrees F (63 degrees C). Remove chops from the skillet, reserving broth mixture, and set aside.

- Step 3

In a bowl, blend the brown sugar, cornstarch, and pineapple juice. Mix into the skillet with the chicken broth mixture. Bring to a boil. Serve with the cooked pork chops.

Eggless Pasta

Ingredients

- 2 cups semolina flour

- ½ teaspoon salt

- ½ cup warm water

Directions

- Step 1

In a large bowl, mix flour and salt. Add warm water and stir to make a stiff dough. Increase water if dough seems too dry.

- Step 2

Pat the dough into a ball and turn out onto a lightly floured surface. Knead for 10 to 15 minutes. Cover. Let dough rest for 20 minutes.

- Step 3

Roll out dough using rolling pin or pasta machine. Work with a 1/4 of the dough at one time. Keep the rest covered, to prevent from drying out. Roll by hand to 1/16 of an inch thick. By machine, stop at the third to last setting.

- Step 4

Cut pasta into desired shapes.

- Step 5

Cook fresh noodles in boiling salted water for 3 to 5 minutes. Drain.

Broccoli Beef I

Ingredients

- ¼ cup all-purpose flour

- 1 (10.5 ounce) can beef broth

- 2 tablespoons white sugar

- 2 tablespoons soy sauce

- 1 pound boneless round steak, cut into bite size pieces

- ¼ teaspoon chopped fresh ginger root

- 1 clove garlic, minced

- 4 cups chopped fresh broccoli

Directions

- Step 1

In a small bowl, combine flour, broth, sugar, and soy sauce. Stir until sugar and flour are dissolved.

- Step 2

In a large skillet or wok over high heat, cook and stir beef 2 to 4 minutes, or until browned. Stir in broth mixture, ginger, garlic, and broccoli. Bring to a boil, then reduce heat. Simmer 5 to 10 minutes, or until sauce thickens.

Cod with Italian Crumb Topping

Ingredients

- ¼ cup fine dry bread crumbs

- 2 tablespoons grated Parmesan cheese

- 1 tablespoon cornmeal

- 1 teaspoon olive oil

- ½ teaspoon Italian seasoning

- ⅛ teaspoon garlic powder

- ⅛ teaspoon ground black pepper

- 4 (3 ounce) fillets cod fillets

- 1 egg white, lightly beaten

Directions

- Step 1

Preheat oven to 450 degrees F (230 degrees C).

- Step 2

In a small shallow bowl, stir together the bread crumbs, cheese, cornmeal, oil, italian seasoning, garlic powder and pepper; set aside.

- Step 3

Coat the rack of a broiling pan with cooking spray. Place the cod on the rack, folding under any thin edges of the filets. Brush with the egg white, then spoon the crumb mixture evenly on top.

- Step 4

Bake in a preheated oven for 10 to 12 minutes or until the fish flakes easily when tested with a fork and is opaque all the way through.

Chickpea Curry

Ingredients

- 2 tablespoons vegetable oil

- 2 onions, minced

- 2 cloves garlic, minced

- 2 teaspoons fresh ginger root, finely chopped

- 6 whole cloves

- 2 (2 inch) sticks cinnamon, crushed

- 1 teaspoon ground cumin

- 1 teaspoon ground coriander

- salt

- 1 teaspoon cayenne pepper

- 1 teaspoon ground turmeric

- 2 (15 ounce) cans garbanzo beans

- 1 cup chopped fresh cilantro

Directions

- Step 1

Heat oil in a large frying pan over medium heat, and fry onions until tender.

- Step 2

Stir in garlic, ginger, cloves, cinnamon, cumin, coriander, salt, cayenne, and turmeric. Cook for 1 minute over medium heat, stirring constantly. Mix in garbanzo beans and their liquid. Continue to cook and stir until all ingredients are well blended and heated through. Remove from heat. Stir in cilantro just before serving, reserving 1 tablespoon for garnish.

Fast and Friendly Meatballs

Ingredients

- 2 tablespoons olive oil

- 1 (20 ounce) package ground turkey

- 1 egg, beaten

- ⅓ cup Italian seasoned bread crumbs

Directions

- Step 1

Preheat the oven to 350 degrees F (175 degrees C). Grease a 9x13 inch baking dish with the olive oil, and place it in the oven while preheating.

- Step 2

In a medium bowl, mix together the ground turkey, egg, and bread crumbs using your hands. Using an ice cream scoop if possible, form the meat into golf ball sized meatballs. Place about 1 inch apart in the hot baking dish. Press down to flatten the bottom just slightly.

- Step 3

Bake for 15 minutes in the preheated oven, then turn them over, and continue baking for about 5 more minutes, or until somewhat crispy on the outside. Serve with pasta and sauce or however you'd like.

Quick Black Beans and Rice

Ingredients

- 1 tablespoon vegetable oil

- 1 onion, chopped

- 1 (15 ounce) can black beans, undrained

- 1 (14.5 ounce) can stewed tomatoes

- 1 teaspoon dried oregano

- ½ teaspoon garlic powder

- 1 ½ cups uncooked instant brown rice

- 1 pound turkey tenderloins

- 3 tablespoons soy sauce

- 1 tablespoon Dijon-style prepared mustard

- 2 teaspoons dried rosemary, crushed

Directions

- Step 1

Place the turkey tenderloins in a sealable plastic bag and set aside.

- Step 2

In a small bowl combine the soy sauce, mustard and rosemary. Pour over turkey, seal bag and shake to coat. Marinate in the refrigerator for 1 to 4 hours shaking once or twice.

- Step 3

Preheat oven on the broiler setting. Remove the turkey from the marinade and place on the rack in the broiler pan. Broil 4 inches from the heat, turning once, for 20 to 22 minutes or until meat is cooked through and when pierced with a fork the juices run clear. Slice and serve with Cranberry Chutney.

Slow Cooker Chicken Marrakesh

Ingredients

- 1 onion, sliced

- 2 cloves garlic, minced (Optional)

- 2 large carrots, peeled and diced

- 2 large sweet potatoes, peeled and diced

- 1 (15 ounce) can garbanzo beans, drained and rinsed

- 2 pounds skinless, boneless chicken breast halves, cut into 2-inch pieces

- ½ teaspoon ground cumin

- ½ teaspoon ground turmeric

- ¼ teaspoon ground cinnamon

- ½ teaspoon ground black pepper

- 1 teaspoon dried parsley

- 1 teaspoon salt

- 1 (14.5 ounce) can diced tomatoes

Directions

- Step 1

Place the onion, garlic, carrots, sweet potatoes, garbanzo beans, and chicken breast pieces into a slow cooker. In a bowl, mix the cumin, turmeric, cinnamon, black pepper, parsley, and salt, and sprinkle over the chicken and vegetables. Pour in the tomatoes, and stir to combine.

- Step 2

Cover the cooker, set to High, and cook until the sweet potatoes are tender and the sauce has thickened, 4 to 5 hours.

Spicy Tuna Sushi Roll

Ingredients

- 2 cups uncooked glutinous white rice

- 2 ½ cups water

- 1 tablespoon rice vinegar

- 1 (5 ounce) can solid white tuna in water, drained

- 1 tablespoon mayonnaise

- 1 teaspoon chili powder

- 1 teaspoon wasabi paste

- 4 sheets nori (dry seaweed)

- ½ cucumber, finely diced

- 1 carrot, finely diced

- 1 avocado - peeled, pitted and diced

Directions

- Step 1

Bring the rice, water, and vinegar to a boil in a saucepan over high heat. Reduce heat to medium-low, cover, and simmer until the rice is tender, and the liquid has been absorbed, 20 to 25 minutes. Let stand, covered, for about 10 minutes to absorb any excess water. Set rice aside to cool.

- Step 2

Lightly mix together the tuna, mayonnaise, chili powder, and wasabi paste in a bowl, breaking the tuna apart but not mashing it into a paste.

- Step 3

To roll the sushi, cover a bamboo sushi rolling mat with plastic wrap. Lay a sheet of nori, rough side up, on the plastic wrap. With wet fingers, firmly pat a thick, even layer of prepared rice over the nori, covering it completely. Place about 1 tablespoon each of diced cucumber, carrot, and avocado in a line along the bottom edge of the sheet, and spread a line of tuna mixture alongside the vegetables.

- Step 4

Pick up the edge of the bamboo rolling sheet, fold the bottom edge of the sheet up, enclosing the filling, and tightly roll the sushi into a thick cylinder. Once the sushi is rolled, wrap it in the mat and gently squeeze to compact it tightly. Cut each roll into 6 pieces, and refrigerate until served.

Bengali Chicken Curry with Potatoes

Ingredients

- 2 tablespoons olive oil

- 2 large onions, diced

- 1 tablespoon ginger-garlic paste

- 2 large tomatoes, diced

- 1 teaspoon cayenne pepper, or more to taste

- 1 teaspoon curry powder

- 1 teaspoon garam masala

- 1 teaspoon ground turmeric

- 1 teaspoon ground cumin

- 4 skinless, boneless chicken breast halves - cut into bite-size pieces

- 2 large red-skinned potatoes, chopped

- ½ cup fresh cilantro

Directions

- Step 1

Heat the olive oil in a large skillet over medium-high heat. Cook and stir the onions in the hot oil until translucent, about 5 minutes. Add the ginger-garlic paste and continue cooking another 5 minutes. Reduce heat to medium; stir the tomatoes into the mixture and cook until the tomatoes are pulpy, 5 to 10 minutes. Season with the cayenne pepper, curry powder, garam masala, turmeric, and cumin; cook and stir another 5 minutes.

- Step 2

Add the chicken and potatoes to the mixture in the skillet; simmer, stirring occasionally, until the potatoes are tender and the chicken is no longer pink in the center, about 20 minutes. Sprinkle the cilantro over the mixture and continue simmering another 10 minutes. Serve hot.

Baked Halibut Steaks

Ingredients

- 1 teaspoon olive oil

- 1 cup diced zucchini

- ½ cup minced onion

- 1 clove garlic, peeled and minced

- 2 cups diced fresh tomatoes

- 2 tablespoons chopped fresh basil

- ¼ teaspoon salt

- ¼ teaspoon ground black pepper

- 4 (6 ounce) halibut steaks

- ⅓ cup crumbled feta cheese

Directions

- Step 1

Preheat oven to 450 degrees F (230 degrees C). Lightly grease a shallow baking dish.

- Step 2

Heat olive oil in a medium saucepan over medium heat and stir in zucchini, onion, and garlic. Cook and stir 5 minutes or until tender. Remove saucepan from heat and mix in tomatoes, basil, salt, and pepper.

- Step 3

Arrange halibut steaks in a single layer in the prepared baking dish. Spoon equal amounts of the zucchini mixture over each steak. Top with feta cheese.

- Step 4

Bake 15 minutes in the preheated oven, or until fish is easily flaked with a fork.

Fra Diavolo Sauce With Pasta

Ingredients

- 4 tablespoons olive oil, divided

- 6 cloves garlic, crushed

- 3 cups whole peeled tomatoes with liquid, chopped

- 1 ½ teaspoons salt

- 1 teaspoon crushed red pepper flakes

- 1 (16 ounce) package linguine pasta

- 8 ounces small shrimp, peeled and deveined

- 8 ounces bay scallops

- 1 tablespoon chopped fresh parsley

Directions

- Step 1

In a large saucepan, heat 2 tablespoons of the olive oil with the garlic over medium heat. When the garlic starts to sizzle, pour in the tomatoes. Season with salt and red pepper. Bring to a boil. Lower the heat, and simmer for 30 minutes, stirring occasionally.

- Step 2

Meanwhile, bring a large pot of lightly salted water to a boil. Cook pasta for 8 to 10 minutes, or until al dente; drain.

- Step 3

In a large skillet, heat the remaining 2 tablespoons of olive oil over high heat. Add the shrimp and scallops. Cook for about 2 minutes, stirring frequently, or until the shrimp turn pink. Add shrimp and scallops to the tomato mixture, and stir in the parsley. Cook for 3 to 4 minutes, or until the sauce just begins to bubble. Serve sauce over pasta.

Printed in Great Britain
by Amazon